International Series on Computer Entertainment and Media Technology

Series Editor
Newton Lee
Tujunga, California, USA

The International Series on Computer Entertainment and Media Technology presents forward-looking ideas, cutting-edge research, and in-depth case studies across a wide spectrum of entertainment and media technology. The series covers a range of content from professional to academic. Entertainment Technology includes computer games, electronic toys, scenery fabrication, theatrical property, costume, lighting, sound, video, music, show control, animation, animatronics, interactive environments, computer simulation, visual effects, augmented reality, and virtual reality. Media Technology includes art media, print media, digital media, electronic media, big data, asset management, signal processing, data recording, data storage, data transmission, media psychology, wearable devices, robotics, and physical computing.

More information about this series at http://www.springer.com/series/13820

Jeff K. T. Tang • Patrick C. K. Hung
Editors

Computing in Smart Toys

 Springer

Editors
Jeff K. T. Tang
School of Computing and Information
    Sciences
Caritas Institute of Higher Education
Tseung Kwan O, Hong Kong

Patrick C. K. Hung
University of Ontario Institute of Technology
Oshawa, ON, Canada

ISSN 2364-947X   ISSN 2364-9488   (electronic)
International Series on Computer Entertainment and Media Technology
ISBN 978-3-319-87227-8   ISBN 978-3-319-62072-5   (eBook)
DOI 10.1007/978-3-319-62072-5

Printed on acid-free paper

This Springer imprint is published by Springer Nature
The registered company is Springer International Publishing AG
The registered company address is: Gewerbestrasse 11, 6330 Cham, Switzerland

Contents

Introduction

Patrick C. K. Hung, Jeff K. T. Tang, and Kamen Kanev

1 Introduction

A toy is an item or product intended for learning or play, which can have various benefits to childhood development. Based on the reporting from the 114th Annual American International Toy Fair at New York, toy manufacturers are increasingly incorporating Artificial Intelligence (AI) functions into their products through the use of mobile software and hardware. A smart toy is defined as a device consisting of a physical toy component that connects to one or more toy computing services to facilitate gameplay in the Cloud through networking and sensory technologies to enhance the functionality of a traditional toy. A smart toy in this context can be effectively considered an Internet of Thing (IoT) with AI functions which can provide Augmented Reality (AR) experiences to users. Examples of these are Mattel's Hello Barbie and Cognitoys' Dino. Toy computing is a recently developing concept which transcends the traditional toy into a new area of computer research using services computing technologies (Hung 2015). In this context, a toy is a physical embodiment artefact that acts as a child user interface for toy computing services. A toy can also capture child user's physical activity state (e.g., walking,

P.C.K. Hung (✉)
Faculty of Business and IT, University of Ontario Institute of Technology, Oshawa, ON, Canada
e-mail: Patrick.Hung@uoit.ca

J.K.T. Tang
School of Computing and Information Sciences, Caritas Institute of Higher Education, Tseung Kwan O, Hong Kong
e-mail: jtang@cihe.edu.hk

K. Kanev
Graduate School of Science and Technology, Shizuoka University, Shizuoka, Japan
e-mail: kanev@rie.shizuoka.ac.jp

© Springer International Publishing AG 2017
J.K.T. Tang, P.C.K. Hung (eds.), *Computing in Smart Toys*, International Series on Computer Entertainment and Media Technology,
DOI 10.1007/978-3-319-62072-5_1

standing, running, etc.) and store personalized information (e.g., location, activity pattern, etc.) through camera, microphone, Global Positioning System (GPS), and various sensors such as facial recognition or sound detection modules. For example, a new invention called the "Google Toy" like a humanoid toy has caused many criticisms from the media as people express concern about possible privacy breaching by Google.

Information privacy is defined by Hung and Cheng (2009) as "an individual's right to determine how, when, and to what extent information about the self will be released to another person or to an organization." As the information disclosure practices are outlined in the privacy policy on smart toys, the parents/guardians are required to provide their consent for their children. However, the parents/guardians are not actually aware of these policies since in fact that they did not read or understand the policy. Content unawareness occurs when the user is unaware of the information that is collected on them, e.g., their location via GPS on the toy. While parents strive to ensure their child's physical and online safety and privacy, they may wish to be in control of how their personal data is shared through the devices they are using (Salomon 2010). Parental control is a feature in a smart toy for the parents to restrict the content the children can provide to the toy (Noor et al. 2012). Thus, there is a need for a privacy quantification that enables the parents/guardians to decide whether to share their children's private data to smart toys. Child users exhibit a varying level of awareness when it comes to their online activities and understanding of privacy risks. Children must be protected from risks which they can be vulnerable to online including violence, harassment, stalking, grooming, sexual abuse or exploitation, or personal data misuse. Furthermore, children also take up a large segment of the consumer population and are of particular interest to market researchers who may attempt to collect their personal data and usage patterns for targeted advertising (Salomon 2010). Third party advertisers can infer a great amount of information about a child based on their location via GPS, collecting detailed behavioral profiles that may be used for unknown or unwanted purposes.

More specifically, the toy makers are confronted with the challenge of better understanding the consumer needs, concerns and exploring the possibility of adopting such context-aware smart toys to rich information interface in this emerging market. For example, Spin Master Inc., which is a Canadian toy company listed in Toronto Stock Exchange (TSE), has been researching the balance between the level of private information a toy collected from a user and the level of personalized features the toy provided to the user. Referring to the direction of the United States Federal Trade Commission Children's Online Privacy Protection Act (COPPA) and the European Union Data Protection Directive (EUDPD), people usually adopt the definition of a child to be an individual under the age of 13 years old. In this research program, the first assumption is that children do not understand the concept of privacy. The second assumption is that children will disclose as much information to smart toys as they can trust. For example, many studies found that specifically anthropomorphic toys like a teddy bears or bunny rabbit serve a purpose, as children trusted such designs and felt at ease disclosing private information. For example, the newly invented human-like "Google Toy" has caused many criticisms from the media as people express concern about possible privacy breaching by Google. As another example, there is a class action lawsuit alleging that Mattel's Hello Barbie records children's conversations without parental consent, in violation of the Children's Online Privacy Protection Act (COPPA) in California (Smiley 2016). Further, Germany's telecommunications watchdog has ordered parents to destroy or disable a "smart doll" because the toy can be used to illegally spy on children.

As smart toys are able to collect variety of data such as text, picture, video, sound, location, and sensing data, this makes the context of toy computing far more complicated than many other smart devices in particular given that the subjects are mainly children in a physical and social environment. Privacy can result in physical safety of child users, e.g., child predators. While the parents/guardians of a child strive to ensure their child's physical and online safety and privacy, there is no common data visualization model with parental control for these parents/guardians to visualize the information flow between their child and the smart toys they interact with. Parental control is a feature in a smart toy for the parents to restrict the content the children can provide to the toy. Though the toy industry has also issued regulations for toy safety, these regulations have no mention of privacy issues in this toy computing paradigm. In particular, it is believed that the smart toys will have advanced software (e.g., face and sound detection algorithms) and hardware (e.g., various sensors) in the coming future.

2 Literature Review

Some research studies found out that children have emotional interactions with dolls and stuffed toys with anthropomorphic designs (Tanaka and Kimura 2009). Some children even prefer to take the toy to the dinner table or make a bed for it next to the child's own (Plowman and Luckin 2004). Toy computing inherits laws and regulations from the components that make it up (e.g., online services and toys), however, there are no laws that explicitly regulate this unique environment of toy computing. There is also no widely adopted common framework to allow parents to monitor and configure the privacy of their children in this paradigm. Children's data is widely considered to be particularly sensitive and should be treated with extreme care by law and legislation. End user requirements need to consider that the main user base is children, who have unique requirements as they are especially vulnerable and in order to protect their sensitive data, parents/guardians require a method to implement privacy controls on their child's data. This research challenge is much greater than many other disciplines as it is a cross-over of toy computing, context data model and privacy technologies with the three principles: (1) Data minimization – minimizing collection and retention of potentially sensitive user data; (2) User participation – allowing parents/guardians to be in control of their child's private data; and (3) Compliance with laws and regulations – the Personal Information Protection and Electronic Documents Act (PIPEDA), United Nations Children's Fund (UNICEF), and COPPA. The Toy Industry Association (TIA) has also raised concerns that restrictions could limit the ability for toy companies to obtain necessary data to analyze and improve content, allow children to enjoy personalized but anonymous online experiences, and benefit from the ability to offer targeted advertising on their e-commerce and adult sites.

3   Book Organization

This book is organized into nine main chapters. Chapter "Pokémon Go: Marketing Implications for Mobile Video Game" discusses a case study of Pokemon Go as a mobile video game from marketing perspective. Chapter "A Survey on Purchase Intention of Hello Barbie in Brazil and Argentina" presents a survey of purchase intention of Hello Barbie in Brazil and Argentina, where consumers still have not been massively presented to this type of smart toy. Chapter "Designing Hand Tracked Exergames with Virtual Toys" outlines the design of a hand tracking exergame using virtual toys as a form to provide the user with suitable interactions with the computer-generated world that require physical activity based on health care exercises. Chapter "Robot Toys for Children with Disabilities" shows some experiments conducted with physically impaired and Autism Spectrum Disorder (ASD) children using qualitative to quantitative scales, which are used to quantify the quality of the experiments and the usability of the robots. Chapter "Towards a Privacy Rule Conceptual Model for Smart Toys" presents a privacy rule conceptual model with the concepts of smart toy, mobile service, device, location, and guidance with related privacy entities: purpose, recipient, obligation, and retention for smart toys. Chapter "Designing for Parental Control: Enriching Usability and Accessibility in the Context of Smart Toys" discusses traditional Human-Computer Interaction methods, with examples focused on Parental Control interfaces in the context of Smart Toys, aiming practitioners from security and privacy area. Chapter "A Security Threat Analysis of Smart Home Network with Vulnerable Dynamic Agents" presents a security analysis of a smart home network containing vulnerable dynamic agents in the form of smart toys. Lastly, Chapter "Privacy Preservation Framework for Smart Connected Toys" proposes some common best practice for parents and toy manufactures can both adopt as part of Smart Connected Toy Privacy Common body of knowledge for child safety.

References

Hung PCK (2015) Mobile services for toy computing, The Springer International series on applications and trends in computer science. Springer International Publishing, Cham

Hung PCK, Cheng V (2009) Privacy. In: Encyclopedia of database systems. Springer, New York, pp 2136–2137

Noor R, Noor Sahila Syed Jamal S, Hafizzee Zakaria K (2012) Parental module control system for children's internet use. 2012 International Conference on Information Society (i-society), London, pp 511–513

Plowman L, Luckin R (2004) Interactivity, interfaces, and smart toys. Computer 37(2):98–100

Salomon D (2010) Privacy and trust. In: Elements of computer security, undergraduate topics in computer science. Springer, London, pp 273–290

Smiley L (2016) When toys talk (and listen). The California Sunday Magazine, September 29, 2016

Tanaka F, Kimura T (2009) The use of robots in early education: a scenario based on ethical consideration. The 18th IEEE International Symposium on Robot and Human Interactive Communication, Toyama, pp 558–560

Pokémon Go: Marketing Implications for Mobile Video Game

Terry Wu

1 Introduction

Children play with toys as part of their growing-up experience. While traditional toys such as dolls, small cars, and action figures are still popular, there has been a gradual shift to toys with digital functions. It is increasingly common to see products that combine the features of traditional toys with computing software and hardware (Dhar and Wu 2015). In recent years, advances in digital technology have enabled gaming companies to produce mobile games for smartphones and tablets.

Mobile gaming is now a big business that was predicted to generate $36.9 billion in 2016 (Newzoo 2016). In the past, gaming companies focused on the traditional consoles where profits were much higher. However, they have noticed the growth potential and global trend of mobile gaming. With a market size of approximately 1.9 billion players worldwide, mobile gaming is becoming a lucrative market. Many gaming companies are moving towards development of mobile games because of the huge market potential. Given the popularity of smartphones and tablets, mobile gaming is now the fastest growing segment in the gaming industry (Newzoo 2016).

One of the most successful mobile games is Pokémon Go, which created a sudden craze around the world in the summer of 2016. Globally, millions of people play this mobile game to find and catch Pokémon characters. It is common to see crowds of players wandering around streets and parks with their smartphones in pursuit of these fictional monster creatures. At the time of writing, this mobile game had been downloaded more than 550 million times globally, with a continuing download of 700,000 a day (Seitz 2016). Even after the initial craze subsided, the game still had 20 million active daily players in the U.S. (Rogers 2016). This game is currently

T. Wu (✉)
Faculty of Business and IT, University of Ontario Institute of Technology, Oshawa, ON, Canada
e-mail: terry.wu@uoit.ca

© Springer International Publishing AG 2017
J.K.T. Tang, P.C.K. Hung (eds.), *Computing in Smart Toys*, International Series on Computer Entertainment and Media Technology,
DOI 10.1007/978-3-319-62072-5_2

available in more than 200 countries, excluding China and North Korea. Pokémon Go is a big money-maker, generating $470 million in the 82 days following its launch (Seitz 2016). At its peak, it brought in $16 million a day. Despite declining popularity, the game continued to generate more than $2 million a day in September 2016 (Seitz 2016).

The purpose of this study is to discuss marketing issues and implications of Pokémon Go. The objective is to use Pokémon Go as a case study to outline the marketing challenges facing a free-to-play mobile game. This study is organized as follows. First, we relate the origins of Pokémon. Next we analyze the operations of Pokémon Go from the perspective of a player. Then we discuss market segmentation and positioning of Pokémon Go. This is followed by a review of the Pokémon Go Life Cycle (PGLC). Finally, we address the marketing implications of this mobile game and provide insights into its success and deficiencies.

2 Pokémon

Pokémon is a video game and trading-card game franchise that was created in 1996 (Gibson 2002). The word Pokémon (ポケモン) is an abbreviation of the Japanese slang term *Pocket Monsters (Poketto Monsuta)* (Bainbridge 2014). It started as a video game for the Game Boy that was developed by Nintendo. It is considered to be one of the most successful video games in the world, after Super Mario (Bainbridge 2014).

The franchise, which is now 20 years old, was created by Satoshi Tajiri in Japan in 1995 (Bainbridge 2014). The Pokémon cast includes many fictional characters such as Pikachu, Charmander, and Squirtle (Barbo 1999; Haiven 2012). There are more than 700 Pokémon characters for the game. These tiny creatures have special powers. Of all the pocket monsters, Pikachu—a cute, yellow, mousey-looking creature—is the most adored among children (Jordan 2004; Nagao 1998; Tobin 2004). The humans are called "trainers" who collect as many Pokémon as possible and fight against other trainers. The best-known slogan for Pokémon is: "Gotta Catch 'Em All" (Buckingham and Sefton-Green 2003). Pokémon has evolved from a Game Boy program to an array of associated products: cartoon, movies, trading cards, video games, comic books, toy figures, and merchandise (Allison 2003, 2006; Jordon 2004). The Pokémon franchise is very lucrative, with total revenue amounting to more than US$46.2 billion in 2016.

Over the last two decades, there has been a great deal of research on Pokémon. In the literature, most studies on Pokémon focus on four themes: commercialization (Buckingham and Sefton-Green 2003; Tobin 2004), consumerism (Allison 2003, 2006), production value (Haiven 2012), and culture (Bainbridge 2014; Jordan 2004). Since both boys and girls like Pokémon, one sociological study focused on the relationship between the role of gender and Pokémon (Ogletree et al. 2004). However, most studies focus on the cultural, sociological, and media aspects. It is surprising that there has been no study on Pokémon in the academic marketing literature. This study is an attempt to fill this research gap.

3 Pokémon Go

Pokémon Go is a mobile augmented reality (AR) game that was released worldwide in July 2016. It is a free-to-play, location-based mobile game that can be downloaded on smartphones (Wingfield and Isaac 2016). The game is simple: its objective is to catch Pokémon created on screen by AR. But the player is encouraged to purchase in-game items in order to access more contents in the game (Wingfield and Isaac 2016). Pokémon Go was created by Niantic and Pokémon Company, which is partially owned by Nintendo (Wingfield and Isaac 2016).

This mobile AR game is a computer-generated information technology that combines video, graphics, and a GPS (global positioning system) tracking system to offer players a live, real-world physical and interactive environment. Smartphones are ideal user interface devices that contain all the requirements for mobile AR applications including a camera, fast Internet connections, and GPS (Olsson and Salo 2011). Pokémon Go is able to use image recognition-based AR (via a camera) on the smartphones to connect the physical world with interactive digital content in a visual display (Olsson and Salo 2011). This mobile game uses the player's actual location in real life. It is common to see players wandering around streets and other city locations (e.g. city parks or downtown landmarks), with their smartphone in hand, at all hours.

Pokémon Go relies on the GPS and Google map to track a player's movement and physical position in an outdoor setting (Wingfield and Isaac 2016). The mobile game app is available for iPhone and Android devices. All the players need to do is to hold the smartphone while pressing the camera button to catch the Pokémon. In order to understand the operations of this mobile game, it is worth discussing several key components of Pokémon Go.

1. **Pokémon characters**

   As in the Pokémon cartoon and video game, players want to collect as many Pokémon as possible. Using their smartphone screens, players walk around their neighborhood to catch the Pokémon and train them (Tsukayama 2016). Locations of Pokémon vary by real geographical locations. Players cannot catch a Pokémon until it is physically near them in the surrounding area. For this mobile game, there are currently a total of 150 Pokémon monsters that players can catch. Most players want to catch rare Pokémon, which are hard to find. Of particular interest is the possibility for trainers to find and hatch an egg for a future Pokémon. Figure 1 shows a Pokémon character known as a Squirtle.

2. **Pokédex**

   The Pokédex is an electronic binder used to record the list of captured Pokémon (Peterson 2016). The concept is similar to an accounting ledger. Thus, the Pokédex shows all the Pokémon that a player has captured so far. A player is automatically registered by the Pokédex when playing the game (see Fig. 2).

   A collection of Pokémon is shown in the Pokédex (see Fig. 3).

Fig. 1 Pokémon

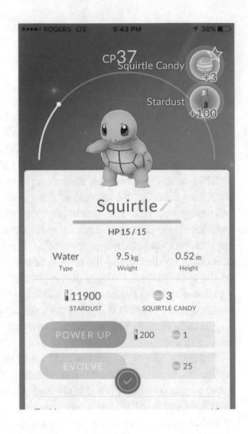

3. Pokéstops

The Pokéstops identify the sites of interest in the real world and offer game items for sale (Sablich 2016). Figure 4 shows the Pokéstop map, which is based on a Google map with the GPS tracking system. A compass is available on the top right side in the Pokéstop. The Pokéstop pops up on the smartphone screen when a player arrives at a location or a site of interest (e.g. a park or a shopping mall).

In some instances, players are lured to Pokéstops that are usually city landmarks or places of interest in the surrounding area. The purpose of the Pokéstops is two-fold. First, each player can obtain items such as Pokéballs or eggs at the Pokéstops to catch Pokémon (Tsukayama 2016). Second, each player can receive for free and use an item to lure Pokémon. For each location, the time duration is limited to 10 minutes at a time. Figure 4 shows the nearby Pokémon in the top right corner.

4. Gyms

Gyms are locations that allow players to battle other players for territories (Tsukayama 2016). For example, a player can kick out an enemy to control the territory. Also, a player can join a faction to compete (Sablich 2016). Figure 5 shows a gym that is located in the Toronto Port Authority.

Fig. 2 Pokédex

4 Segmentation and Positioning

Most companies use a segmentation strategy for marketing consumer products. Marketers tend to group consumers into different market segments with specific needs and desires (Barron and Hollingshead 2002; Dickson and Ginter 1987). A practical segmentation strategy may result in increased revenues and higher profits.

Game companies are no exception. It is reasonable to expect that gamers come from diverse backgrounds with different needs, wants, attitudes, and habits (Ip and Jacobs 2005). This is why it is important to know the types of games played by specific players in the marketplace. In general, marketers use several dimensions to segment the video game market, as detailed below.

1. **Demographic segmentation**

    This is a commonly used method to segment a market based on demographic characteristics such as gender, age, race, and income (Cleveland et al. 2011). It is likely that men and women play different video games due to differences in attitudes and behaviors (Fisher and Dube 2005). Similarly, players are likely to play different games at different ages. For example, young children may prefer to play Super Mario, whereas young adults may prefer Call of Duty.

Fig. 3 Collection of
Pokémon in Pokédex

2. **Geographic segmentation**

Another approach to segmentation is based on factors relevant to consumers' locations, such as climates, cultures, histories, countries, regions, and cities (Kahle 1986; Musyoka et al. 2007). For example, Canadians may prefer to play a video game focused on hockey because it is the national sport of Canada. In contrast, soccer is popular in Brazil. So Brazilians may choose a soccer game over hockey. Both soccer and hockey games are created by Electronic Arts Inc. (EA Games).

3. **Psychographic segmentation**

This dimension utilizes consumer behavior indicators of personality and lifestyle to segment a consumer market (Kotler et al. 2013; Tigert et al. 1971). Hence, psychographic segmentation creates homogeneous groupings of players based on the objectives, values, and benefits they seek to fulfill (File and Prince 1996). As far as lifestyle is concerned, people who like exercises are likely to play sport-related video games.

4. **Behavioural segmentation**

A marketer uses behavioural segmentation to divide a market based on consumer behaviour in terms of usage rate and loyalty status (Bonn et al. 1999). It is expected that video game players can be grouped into two segments: hard-core

Fig. 4 Pokéstop

players and casual players (Ip and Jacobs 2005). In other words, hard-core gamers play video games all the time, whereas casual gamers play occasionally. It is reasonable to assume that gaming companies develop some games that are specifically targeted at hard-core players.

Most video games are positioned for a particular segment of players (Ip and Jacobs 2005). What is surprising is that Pokémon Go is so successful in attracting so many different segments. This mobile game was initially targeted at teenagers and young adults. Word of mouth and social media were instrumental in spreading this game to the public on a global scale. The game has become so popular that it is no longer confined to any particular segment. This mobile game is played by people of all ages, both sexes, and in many countries. In essence, Pokémon Go is a one-product game for multiple segments, including a large number of hard-core and casual gamers around the world.

Fig. 5 Gym

5 Pokémon Go Life Cycle (PGLC)

The evolution of a consumer product can be best analyzed by means of the product
life cycle theory. The model postulates that a consumer product goes through four
stages of its life: introduction, growth, maturity, and decline (Cox 1967; Grantham
1997; Kotler et al. 2013). The product life cycle theory is used as a management
tool for developing product strategies. It should be noted that the length of each stage
varies from product to product. In other words, the nature of the product affects each
stage. Some products have a long growth period, whereas others have a relatively
short time span to maturity. Each stage requires different strategies in terms of
promotion and distribution (Grantham 1997). Although most products would be
replaced when they are in decline, some products could be revitalized or expanded
during the growth stage or possibly even once they have entered a decline.

   Like conventional toys, most video games do not last for a long time. Players
are attracted to certain games because of the new content and experience (Morlock
et al. 1985). In general, players play a new game when it is first launched, then
stop playing the game after a while. Most games do have a definite life cycle. Some

Fig. 6 Pokémon Go Life
Cycle (PGLC)

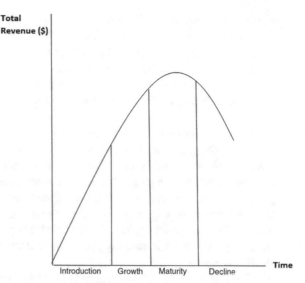

games retain their popularity longer than others, but all games follow similar cycles of launch and fade-out (Zackariasson and Dymek 2017).

Pokémon Go was first launched in Australia, New Zealand, and the United States in early July 2016. But some players in other countries were not ready to wait. They created dummy accounts in order to access the mobile game apps in other countries before the official launch in their home countries. However, the craze did not last long.

Like other video games, Pokémon Go went through four different stages of a life cycle (Cox 1967; Grantham 1997; Kotler et al. 2013). The Pokémon Go Life Cycle (PGLC) is shown in Fig. 6.

1. **Introduction stage**

    The first stage of the PGLC, the introduction, is the birth of the Pokémon Go game. This is a short time period to establish market position early (Cox 1967). After the game was launched in July 2016, Pokémon Go attracted a large number of players to this real-life, location-based mobile game that offered the novelty of reality. There was a high degree of consumer awareness at this stage. The interactive virtual reality game excited players for product trial. Within a short time period, Pokémon Go was able to establish a strong market position. Many of these players were innovators and early adopters.

2. **Growth stage**

    For most products, this is a crucial stage that affects sales through brand growth and market response (Shankar et al. 1999). Given the popularity of this interactive Pokémon Go game immediately after launch, more players were attracted in August, creating a rapid growth period for the game because a huge number of people (mostly gamers) wanted to play it. There was a spillover effect when people saw both friends and strangers chasing Pokémon on their smartphones around city streets. The demand for this game was huge, as there were no other competitors in the marketplace. Players who first tried Pokémon Go were satisfied and then played again to catch more Pokémon. The success of this game is illustrated by its wide distribution on a global scale. By all accounts, the game of Pokémon Go has exceeded all expectations.

3. **Maturity stage**

For most products, the maturity stage occurs when revenue stabilizes and profit declines (Lee et al. 1993; Mason 1976). This was a slow-down phase for the Pokémon Go growth. Within a short period of time, Pokémon Go had attracted even non-gamers such as adults and seniors interested in trying this new mobile game. But some players tried the game and decided to leave it because there were no new versions or new features added. These later players did not usually play other mobile computing games. They played this game because their friends and children played it. This maturity phase was relatively short, around 4–5 weeks.

4. **Decline stage**

After 3 months of continuous growth, Pokémon Go started to lose gamers in October and November 2016. There were no new features or contents added to the game. While some gamers still play Pokémon Go, a large portion started to abandon this game altogether. This is a period of decline for the game when the interest starts to wear off. From a marketing perspective, players in this category were laggards.

It is interesting to note that the duration for the first two stages (introduction and growth) was around 2 months. In fact, Pokémon Go moved from the introduction stage to maturity in only 3 months. Like other fads, Pokémon Go experienced a rapid growth and then a rapid decline. As shown in Fig. 6, Pokémon Go follows the pattern of other short life-cycle technology products, depicting a single modal curve with growth, maturity, and decline stages (Aytac and Wu 2011). The problem with Pokémon Go is that there were only minor fixes in the game. To stop further decline, Pokémon Go is now starting to add more content. But these changes were too slow in coming to keep most players. For this free-to-play mobile game, the length of the product life cycle is relatively short. It is reasonable to assume that the PGLC could be lengthened to a year or two if there were improved versions of this game with new features.

6   Marketing Implications

The popularity of Pokémon Go offers a golden opportunity for marketers. This game is played by people around the world. At the game's peak in August of 2016, there were more than 21 million active players every day in the U.S. It is a game for all ages and genders. Some businesses were able to benefit from the sudden craze by luring customers to their shops and locations. Marketers have adopted the following tactics to take advantage of the game's popularity.

1. **Sales promotion**

   The unique feature of Pokémon Go is that players are required to physically walk around to catch Pokémon. This allows businesses to lure gamers to their locations to play. For example, some businesses offer free Wi-Fi to catch Pokémon, whereas some bars offer a discount after a customer shows a picture of catching a Pokémon nearby. The purpose is to drive foot traffic to their businesses. In August 2016, for example, Toronto Zoo launched a promotional in-game event by inviting players to attend a Pokémon Go Party at its location, where there was a total of 45 Pokéstops and 4 gyms (*Scarborough Mirror* 2016).

2. **Partnerships/Sponsorships**

   A business can form a strategic partnership by sponsoring the Pokémon Go game (Wingfield and Isaac 2016). In essence, marketers can advertise their products and services in Pokémon Go as part of the mobile game on the phone screen. Also, businesses could offer either monetary rewards (e.g. discounts) or free sample coupons to players. In Japan, McDonald's and Softbank Mobile are two major paid sponsors for Pokémon Go (Mochizuki 2016). All the 3000 McDonald's restaurants are designated as Pokémon gyms in Japan.

3. **Location-based advertising**

   The interactive Pokémon Go game is based on real-life locations that are listed as the Pokéstops. It is possible for retailers, shops, and restaurants to lure customers to their businesses if the Pokéstops are located nearby. It is important for businesses to avoid sending advertisement alerts to targeted recipients over their phones. This type of unwarranted advertisement could be annoying to some gamers.

7 Conclusions

In many ways, Pokémon Go is similar to a scavenger hunt. Players are supposed to find the Pokémon creatures in different locations. The initial success of Pokémon Go is due to four main factors. First, this mobile game is based on the real-world physical environment with real street names and real buildings on a Google map. Players are addicted to the engaging experience due to the user-generated gameplay. Second, it struck a chord among many of the early adopters who grew up in the era when Pokémon was introduced in the 1990s. The nostalgia effect allows millennial players to relate to the Pokémon game that they were very familiar with when growing up. Third, Pokémon Go has created a type of interaction and gathering for many families when parents and children walk around and play this mobile game together. While demographic segmentation is appropriate for many consumer products (Cleveland et al. 2011; Lin 2002), demographic variables are not successful in identifying useful segment(s) of Pokémon Go players, which include all ages, genders, races, and income levels. Fourth, it was perfect timing for Pokémon Go to be released in the summer when children were out of school. Hence, the game was able to reach a peak demand when millions of school children played it during their summer vacation.

Although Pokémon Go was a popular game, it died down after a short span. Players were tired of playing the same game again and again. There were growing demands for a new version and new features during the maturity stage. Unfortunately, the game company did not listen to players and respond accordingly. Although many gamers expected an improved version to come along, a new version has yet to materialize. One reason is that Pokémon Go is not fully developed yet.

The spectacular success of Pokémon Go was a breakthrough for AR games. For Niantic, it was an adoption of technological innovation that became the firm's competitive advantage (Agarwal and Wu 2015). With such technologies in AR, players are able to use a smartphone to catch Pokémon in a real-world environment. This mobile game has gone through the typical product life cycle with introduction, growth, maturity, and decline phases. It appears that Pokémon Go moved very rapidly from stage to stage over a period of several months. By October 2016, Pokémon Go started to lose gamers. In the future, Pokémon Go needs to evolve beyond the basic features to create an improved version for all players. While Pokémon Go is currently in a period of decline, it is possible to revitalize the brand back to rapid growth and maturity stages if an improved version is available soon.

References

Agarwal J, Wu T (2015) Factors influencing growth potential of E-commerce in emerging economies: an institution-based N-OLI framework and research propositions. Thunderbird Int Bus Rev 57(3):197–215

Allison A (2003) Portable monsters and commodity cuteness: Pokémon as Japan's new global power. Postcolonial Stud 6(3):381–395

Allison A (2006) Millennial monsters: Japanese toys and the global imagination. University of California Press, Berkeley

Aytac B, Wu SD (2011) Modelling high-tech product life cycles with short-term demand information: a case study. J Oper Res Soc 62(3):425–432

Bainbridge J (2014) 'It is Pokémon world': the Pokémon franchise and the environment. Int J Cult Stud 17(4):399–414

Barbo MS (1999) The official Pokémon handbook. Scholastic, New York

Barron J, Hollingshead J (2002) Making segmentation work. Mark Manag 11(1):24–28

Bonn MA, Furr HL, Susskind AM (1999) Predicting a behavioral profile for pleasure travelers on the basis of internet use segmentation. J Travel Res 37(4):333–340

Buckingham D, Sefton-Green J (2003) 'Gotta catch 'em all': structure, agency, and pedagogy in children's media culture. Media Cult Soc 25:379–399

Cleveland M, Papadopoulos N, Laroche M (2011) Identity, demographics, and consumer behaviors: international market segmentation across product categories. Int Mark Rev 28(3):244–266

Cox WE (1967) Product life cycles as marketing models. J Bus 40(4):375–384

Dhar T, Wu T (2015) Mobile computing toys: marketing challenges and implications. In: Hung P (ed) Mobile services for toy computing: the springer international series on applications and trends in computer science. Springer International Publishing AG, Switzerland, pp 39–49

Dickson PR, Ginter JL (1987) Market segmentation, product differentiation, and marketing strategies. J Mark 51(2):1–10

File KM, Prince RA (1996) A psychographic segmentation of industrial family businesses. Ind Mark Manag 25(3):223–234

Fisher RJ, Dube L (2005) Gender differences in responses to emotional advertising: a social desirability perspective. J Consum Res 31(4):850–858

Gibson M (2002) The powers of the Pokémon: histories of television, histories of the concept of power. Media Int Australia 104(2002):107–115

Grantham LM (1997) The validity of the product life cycle in the high-tech industry. Mark Intell Plan 15(1):4–10

Haiven M (2012) Can Pikachu save Fannie Mae? Value, finance and imagination in the new pokeconomy. Cult Stud 26(4):516–541

Ip B, Jacobs G (2005) Segmentation of the games market using multivariate analysis. J Target Meas Anal Mark 13(3):275–287

Jordan T (2004) The pleasures and pains of Pikachu. Eur J Cult Stud 7(4):461–480

Kahle LR (1986) The nine nations of North America and the value basis of geographic segmentation. J Mark 50(2):37–47

Kotler P, Keller KL, Sivaramakrishnan S, Cunningham PH (2013) Marketing Management, 14th Canadian edn. Pearson, Toronto

Lee M, Lee I-K, Ulgado FM (1993) Marketing strategies for mature products in a rapidly developing country: a contingency approach. Int Mark Rev 10(5):56–72

Lin C-F (2002) Segmenting customer brand preference: demographic or psychographic. J Prod Brand Manag 11(4/5):249–268

Mason RS (1976) Product maturity and marketing strategy. Eur J Mark 10(1):36–48

Mochizuki T (2016) McDonald's Japan unit plans Pokémon go tic-up. Wall Street Journal, July 20, 2016

Morlock H, Yando T, Nigolean K (1985) Motivation of video game players. Psychol Rep 57(1):247–250

Musyoka SM, Mutyauvyu SM, Kiema JBK, Karanja FN, Siriba DN (2007) Market segmentation using geographic information systems (GIS): a case study of the soft drink industry in Kenya. Mark Intell Plan 25(6):632–642

Nagao T (1998) Pokemon wa kodomo no teki ka mikata ka? (Is Pokemon the enemy or ally of children?). Koseido Shuppan, Tokyo

Newzoo (2016) Games market trend reports. https://ntsewzoo.com/insights/segments/mobile/ (Retrieved on December 6, 2016)

Ogletree SM, Martinez CN, Turner TR, Mason B (2004) Pokémon: exploring the role of gender. Sex Roles 50(11/12):851–859

Olsson T, Salo M (2011) Online user survey on current mobile augmented reality applications. In: 10th IEEE international symposium on mixed and augmented reality 2011 science and technology proceedings. IEEE, Basel, pp 75–84

Peterson A (2016) How Pokémon go took over my life – and improved it. Washington Post, September 16, 2016. https://www.washingtonpost.com/news/the-switch/wp/2016/09/16/how-pokemon-go-took-over-my-life-and-improved-it/?utm_term=.4b254242c9fe

Rogers C (2016) What next for Pokémon Go? Marketing Week, November 17

Sablich J (2016) Let Pokémon go be your tour guide. New York Times, July 11, 2016. http://www.nytimes.com/2016/07/13/travel/pokemon-go-nyc-tourism.html

Scarborough Mirror (2016) Toronto Zoo Hosts Pokémon Go Party This Weekend for Players to 'Catch 'em All' http://www.insidetoronto.com/whatson-story/6795303-toronto-zoo-hosts-pokemon-go-party-this-weekend-for-players-to-catch-em-all-/

Seitz P (2016) 'Pokemon Go' Still Raking in $2 Million a Day. Investors Business Daily, September 9

Shankar V, Carpenter GS, Krishnamurthi L (1999) The advantages of entry in the growth stage of the product life cycle: an empirical analysis. J Mark Res 36(2):269–276

Tigert DJ, Lathrope R, Bleeg M (1971) The fast food franchise: psychographic and demographic segmentation analysis. J Retail 47(1):81–90

Tobin JJ (2004) Pikachu's global adventure: the rise and fall of Pokémon. Duke University Press, Durham

Tsukayama H (2016) The non-gamer's guide to playing Pokémon go. Washington Post, July 11, 2016. https://www.washingtonpost.com/news/the-switch/wp/2016/07/11/the-non-gamers-guide-to-playing-pokemon-go/?utm_term=.71018852b113

Wingfield N, Isaac M (2016) Pokémon Go Brings Augmented Reality to a Mass Audience. New York Times, July 11, 2016. http://www.nytimes.com/2016/07/12/technology/pokemon-go-brings-augmented-reality-to-a-mass-audience.html?_r=0

Zackariasson P, Dymek M (2017) Video game marketing: a student textbook. Routledge, Abingdon

A Survey on Purchase Intention of Hello Barbie in Brazil and Argentina

Marcelo Fantinato, Patrick C. K. Hung, Ying Jiang, Jorge Roa,
Pablo Villarreal, Mohammed Melaisi, and Fernanda Amancio

1 Introduction

Toys have been a part of human existence for thousands of years, across every culture, being uncovered from as far back as ancient Egyptian times. Toys always reflect the culture in which they are used at that particular time (Byrne 2006). A toy is an item or product intended for learning or play, which can have various benefits to childhood development. Toys can have a variety of purposes including education, leisure, and socialization. The nature of toys is usually used to prepare children for the world they will inhabit as adults (Byrne 2006). As such a substantial part of the human development, toys have continued to maintain a presence in the daily lives of billions of individuals of all ages. While primitive toys included rocks and pinecones, they soon progressed into dolls, stuffed animals and trains. As new ideas continue to develop to reflect the era and culture, it becomes evident that the toy is a product which has evolved along with humankind. It has become a marketable product, which has blossomed into a multi-billion-dollar industry. Electronic toys have gained popularity, consisting of electronic parts with embedded systems. In the past few decades, electronic toys such as Speak & Spell, Tamagotchi, and Furby had become popular. More recently, sensors, and networking capabilities

M. Fantinato (✉) • F. Amancio
School of Arts, Sciences and Humanities, University of São Paulo, São Paulo, Brazil
e-mail: m.fantinato@usp.br; f.amancio@usp.br

P.C.K. Hung • Y. Jiang • M. Melaisi
Faculty of Business and IT, University of Ontario Institute of Technology, Oshawa, ON, Canada
e-mail: patrick.hung@uoit.ca; ying.jiang@uoit.ca; mohammed.melaisi@uoit.ca

J. Roa • P. Villarreal
CIDISI-UTN-CONICET, Santa Fe, Argentina
e-mail: jroa@frsf.utn.edu.ar; pvillarr@frsf.utn.edu.ar

© Springer International Publishing AG 2017
J.K.T. Tang, P.C.K. Hung (eds.), *Computing in Smart Toys*, International Series
on Computer Entertainment and Media Technology,
DOI 10.1007/978-3-319-62072-5_3

have introduced a variety of new possibilities for the toy industry. Toy companies have embraced modern technologies such as mobile devices into the design of their products, reshaping the concept of toys and education through mobile applications and augmented reality.

Children's toys have become increasingly sophisticated over the years, with a growing shift from simple physical products to toys that engage the digital world through software and hardware. A smart toy is defined as a device consisting of a physical toy component that connects to a computing system with online services through networking to enhance the functionality of a traditional toy such as Mattel's Hello Barbie. Barbie is a famous fashion doll sold all over the world. Hello Barbie is introduced as "the first fashion doll that can have a two-way conversation with girls" with speech recognition and Cloud computing technologies. While the doll is made by Mattel Inc., the online English conversation software is powered by a company called ToyTalk. Currently Hello Barbie is only available in the United States of America (USA) market. The targeted players are 7–13 years old children, especially to girls. Adding the ability of speech recognition and online connection raises the risk of a possible privacy breach in children. Since its introduction in February 2015, Hello Barbie has been criticized for the negative effects on children along with privacy concerns (Michael and Hayes 2015). In December 2015, Mattel was sued in California by two mothers to allege that Hello Barbie records their daughter's conversations without parental consent, in violation of the Children's Online Privacy Protection Act (COPPA) in the USA. The United States Federal Trade Commission's COPPA protects the online privacy of children under the age of 13, and indicates that a child's personal information cannot be collected without parental consent. In 2010, an amendment to COPPA further elaborated that personal information includes geolocation information, photographs, and videos. Up to this moment, this case is still under the court in California. Recently the Federal Network Agency (Bundesnetzagentur) in Germany is telling parents to abandon Internet-connected smart toys designed for their kids because of its unsecure and hackable structure that could reveal personal information (Dudau 2017).

Argentina and Brazil are two key economies in South America, both being strategic partners of the MERCOSUR (Common Market of the South). Argentina is the 47th largest export economy in the world and the 43rd most complex economy according (OCE 2017), whereas Brazil is the 23rd largest export economy in the world and the 32nd most complex economy. The top export and import destinations of Argentina are Brazil, China, and the USA (OCE 2017). The top export and import destinations of Brazil are China, the USA, and Argentina (OCE 2017). Up to this moment, Hello Barbie is not ready on the market in South America yet. This study aims to investigate whether the consumers in Argentina and Brazil are ready to accept Hello Barbie in their future toy market. The main objective of this paper is to examine consumers' perception of Hello Barbie (i.e., perceived innovativeness, perception of the conversational function, and perceived risks of the conversational function), their overall evaluation and attitude, and their purchase intention toward Hello Barbie in both Brazil and Argentina. Specifically, we tested whether Brazilian and Argentina consumers perceive Hello Barbie differently and how their perception influences their purchase intention toward the toy. We built our current research on the literature of consumer new product adoption, culture differences among countries, and the effect of culture on new product diffusion. This paper is organized as follows: Section 2 provides background information, Section 3 describes the empirical study in Brazil and Argentina, and Sect. 5 concludes the paper with future work.

2 Background Information

Since Mattel introduced Barbie as a fashion doll icon in early 1959, the doll has been selling over 800 million units around the world (A&E Networks 2016). This popularity faced with concerns among parents such as promoting an unhealthy image of beauty (Hains 2014). In 1991, an electronic product called Teen Talk Barbie, which could speak four phrases out of 270 phrases created by Mattel. One of those phrases was "Math class is tough." Because of this, Mattel received numerous complaints from the American Association of University Women, the National Council of Teachers of Mathematics, and other similar groups. From this example, one can see that the conversation content, which Barbie can speak, is a very critical point to make the doll success or failure in the market. These criticisms and concerns continued with Hello Barbie, which is a Smart Toy manufactured by Mattel (2015). While the doll is made by Mattel Inc., the online conversation software is powered by ToyTalk. ToyTalk has previously released a smartphone application known as SPEAKALEGEND, which allowed children to interact and engage in conversation with imaginary characters such as Unicorn, Mermaid, and Bigfoot (ToyTalk 2015). With their expertise in this field, Mattel cooperated with them to develop the software behind an interactive Hello Barbie. Referring to the vocabulary of Hello Barbie as of November 17, 2015, she can speak 56,367 total words and 3935 unique word forms in 8000 phrases. For example, there is a phrase saying, "Hey, I love math, too. What have you been learning in math class recently?" We believe that this is the lesson Mattel learned from Teen Talk Barbie's case.

Referring to Fig. 1, the children interact with Hello Barbie equipped with Wifi, microphone and speaker in a physical and social environment. When Hello Barbie turns on, the system inside the doll will check if the doll has been linked to a ToyTalk.com account via Wifi. In the parental control, the parents/guardians have to download a mobile application called "Hello Barbie Companion App" on a smart phone to configure the Wifi settings. The ToyTalk.com account provides the parents/guardians functions to manage the conversation option. Following that, the app will ask the parents/guardians for their consent to allow the company to use their child's information, such as voices, their birthday, and holidays they care about. If the parents refuse to give permission, ToyTalk.com will not store any information in the Cloud and the account will be deleted in reasonable time. If the parents give permission to ToyTalk.com, ToyTalk.com will have the right under their privacy policy to gather information from Hello Barbie or even other smart

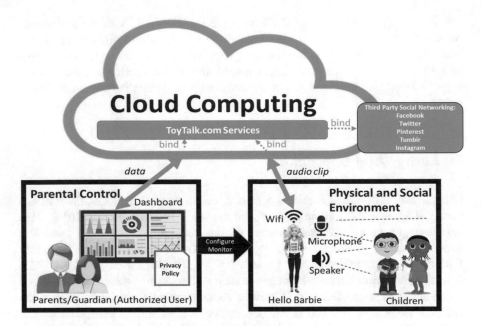

Fig. 1 Conceptual model of Hello Barbie and ToyTalk.com

toys to the account. The conversation options allow the parents to provide the doll with the information of child that is using the doll. The information consists of important holidays, which such as Halloween, Thanksgiving, Christmas, Diwali and Hanukkah. Parents can also provide the child's day and month of birth to Hello Barbie. These options do not require the doll to be in connection mode, which means that the data will be stored in the doll internally through ToyTalk.com services. The physical interface between a child and a smart toy usually is via a touch, e.g., digital button (Goldstein et al. 2004). After this point, the child should be able to engage in conversation with Hello Barbie via a button, while the parents can access the conversation audio clips via the ToyTalk.com account. Hello Barbie will send the collected voice in audio clips to ToyTalk.com services, and ToyTalk.com can bind with other third party social networking services such as Facebook, Twitter, Pinterest, Tumblr and Instagram, in the Cloud. Both Mattel and ToyTalk.com have its own privacy policy that outlines information including how it will collect, manage, share, and retain the user's personal data.

Referring to Fig. 2, ToyTalk.com services on the Cloud has a list of phrases that Hello Barbie is the one who is asking question and waiting for response. After that, Hello Barbie will request a phrase from ToyTalk's services and play an audio response for the user. For the first phrase requested by Hello Barbie, ToyTalk.com will check if the current day matches a day that been marked on the conversation options such as the birthday or a holiday. In such case, some phrases have been linked directly to these special days. For example, Hello Barbie will sing a happy birthday song to the child if today is his/her birthday. There also some

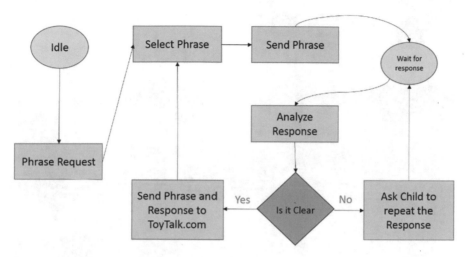

Fig. 2 Hello Barbie phrase conversation

topic related to these days. For example, Hello Barbie will ask the child how it feels being a year older or what he/she did in his birthday. The conversations vary from talking about specific topics such as fashion, school, friends, and family, to playing games and listening to interactive stories. In addition, Hello Barbie will try to ask the user questions regarding these topics to engage them in the conversation. For example, the phrase "Well, we've been talking so much about school... what about all the things we can do when we're not in class? Let's talk about that!" will change the topic from talking about school to talk about hobbies or other interest. In this scenario, one can see that Hello Barbie may actively drive the flow of the conversation.

Referring to Fig. 3, the speech recognition services on ToyTalk.com will receive the child's recording and analyze it to find the best response. Many conditions control the flow of the conversation. In the beginning, ToyTalk.com will check if the user has said phrases or words from a priority list. This list contains of command phrases, such as volume up and down, which make Hello Barbie repeats the last statement in a lower or higher voice. Other phrases include phrases to ask Hello Barbie questions such as "Can I ask you a question?" Another type of conversation is narrative interactive story. In this scenario, Hello Barbie will give the child two options to choose. If the child's answer was vague, Hello Barbie will ask the child again. If the child does not answer clearly for the second time, Hello Barbie will assume one option and carry on with her own story. In a regular topic conversation, Hello Barbie will say something and then ask the child related questions, such as what food they like, how they dressed for an event, what they like about school, etc. In this type of conversation, Hello Barbie asks general questions and does not change her behavior based on the answer. Hello Barbie will remember a few things, such as whether or not if the child has a pet. Another thing Hello Barbie can remember is the last conversation or a previous game played with the user a

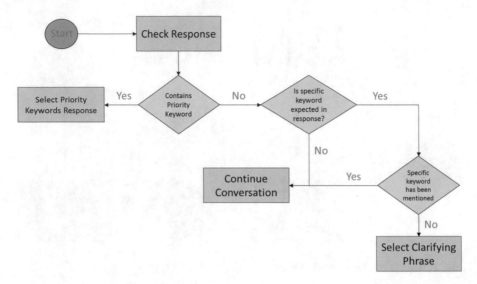

Fig. 3 Hello Barbie keyword interaction

specific topic, in which case Hello Barbie will say something similar to "Do you remember when we did this?" This kind of memory might help to strengthen the connection between Hello Barbie and the user. There are also some phrases that have been stored in Hello Barbie's internal memory to provide an audio feedback of the system. For example, Hello Barbie will ask the user to charge the doll if the battery is low and the doll will say goodbye when the system shuts down.

3   Research Framework

Previous research shows that consumers' purchase intention towards a new product can be influenced by various factors such as consumers' perceived innovativeness, perceived risk, and perceived benefits of the product (Hoeffler 2003; Jhang et al. 2012). When consumers perceive a technology as really new rather than incrementally new, they may find it difficult to understand and appreciate the benefits of the product and thus more likely to fucus on the risks of the product (e.g., Moreau et al. 2001), which then negatively affects consumers' purchase intention toward the product (Hoeffler 2003; Jhang et al. 2012). The conversational function of Hello Barbie is a new innovation applied in children's toys. It can be considered relatively new as not many toys on the market carry the recording and conversational function. However, it does resembles the features of many voice recognition function of adult mobile apps. Therefore, how new consumers perceive

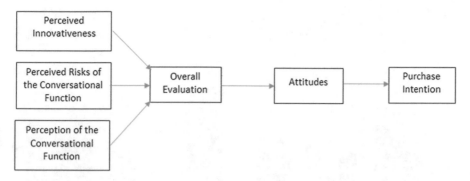

Fig. 4 Proposed research model

Hello Barbie may influence their evaluation of the toy, their attitude toward the toy, and their willingness to purchase the toy for a child. We propose that consumers' perceived innovativeness of the toy, perceived risks of the conversational function, and perception of the conversational function influence their overall evaluation of the toy, attitude toward the toy, and purchase intention toward the toy. Figure 4 depicts our proposed research model.

The existing literature also recognize the effect of cultural difference and social contagion on consumer new product adoption process in different countries (e.g., Van den Bulte and Stremersch 2004). Particularly, they have found four dimensions of Hofstede's national culture dimensions influence new product diffusion curves. These dimensions are uncertainty avoidance, power distance, individualism, and masculinity. Although Brazil and Argentina are the two neighbouring countries in South America, each posesses its unique culture. Figure 5 shows their culture difference along Hofstede's culture dimensions in Table 1. First, uncertainty avoidance is "the extent to which the members of a culture feel threatened by uncertain or unknown situations" (Hofstede 2001). Therefore, consumers in countries with high uncertainty avoidance scores are less likely to adopt new innovations given their risk avoidance nature. Brazil scores 76 and Argentina scores 86 on the uncertainty avoidance dimension. Based on this comparison, we argue that Brazilian consumers are more likely to adopt Hello Barbie than Argentinian consumers. Second, power distance addresses "the extent to which the less powerful members of a culture expect and accept that power is distributed unequally." (Hofstede 2001). Research shows that people in high power distance countries are likely to buy products for its social status and immitate the behaviour of other people. As Brazil scores 69 and Argentina scores 49 on the power distance dimention, we again expect Brazilian consumers are more likely to adopt Hello Barbie than Argentinian consumers. Third, individualism is "the extent to which people from birth onwards are integrated into strong, cohesive in-groups" (Hofstede 2001). People in low individualism cultures, i.e., high collectivism cultures, are likely to adopt new products due to social norm,

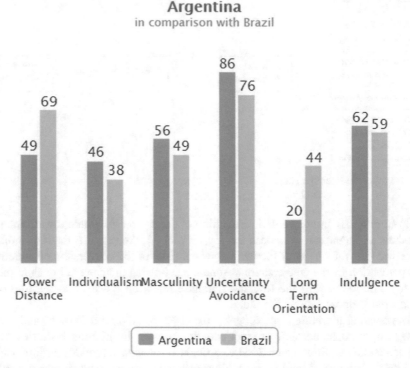

Fig. 5 A comparison of Argentina and Brazil (Adapted from: https://geert-hofstede.com/countries.html)

in other words the pressure to purchase the product just like other people. Brazil scores 38 and Argentinian scores 46 on the individualism dimention. Therefore, we predict that Brazilian consumers are more likely to adopt Hello Barbie than Argentina consumers. Lastly, masculinity is the extent to which "social gender roles are clearly distinct: men are supposed to be assertive, tough, and focused on material success; women are supposed to be more modest, tender, and concerned with the quality of life" (Hofstede 2001). As Brazil scores 49 and Argentina scores 56 on the masculinity dimention, Argentinian consumers may be more interested in acquiring material possessions. However, at the same time, a low masculinity score for Brazil may indicate Brazilians care more about their quality of life. Parents often buy toys to make their children happy and learn new things. Therefore, we cannot predict the difference in adoption based on the masculinity dimension. Overall, as three of the four dimensions suggest that Brazilian consumers are more likely to adopt new products, we predict that Brazilian consumers will evaluate Hello Barbie more positively and have a higher purchase intention toward the toy.

Table 1 Cultural dimension by Hofstede (2001)

Cultural dimension	Description
Power Distance Index (PDI)	This dimension expresses the degree to which the less powerful members of a society accept and expect that power is distributed unequally. The fundamental issue here is how a society handles inequalities among people. People in societies exhibiting a large degree of Power Distance accept a hierarchical order in which everybody has a place and which needs no further justification. In societies with low Power Distance, people strive to equalise the distribution of power and demand justification for inequalities of power.
Individualism versus Collectivism (IDV)	The high side of this dimension, called individualism, can be defined as a preference for a loosely-knit social framework in which individuals are expected to take care of only themselves and their immediate families. Its opposite, collectivism, represents a preference for a tightly-knit framework in society in which individuals can expect their relatives or members of a particular in-group to look after them in exchange for unquestioning loyalty. A society's position on this dimension is reflected in whether people's self-image is defined in terms of "I" or "we."
Masculinity versus Femininity (MAS)	The Masculinity side of this dimension represents a preference in society for achievement, heroism, assertiveness and material rewards for success. Society at large is more competitive. Its opposite, femininity, stands for a preference for cooperation, modesty, caring for the weak and quality of life. Society at large is more consensus-oriented. In the business context Masculinity versus Femininity is sometimes also related to as "tough versus tender" cultures.
Uncertainty Avoidance Index (UAI)	The Uncertainty Avoidance dimension expresses the degree to which the members of a society feel uncomfortable with uncertainty and ambiguity. The fundamental issue here is how a society deals with the fact that the future can never be known: should we try to control the future or just let it happen? Countries exhibiting strong UAI maintain rigid codes of belief and behaviour and are intolerant of unorthodox behaviour and ideas. Weak UAI societies maintain a more relaxed attitude in which practice counts more than principles.
Long Term Orientation versus Short Term Normative Orientation (LTO)	Every society has to maintain some links with its own past while dealing with the challenges of the present and the future. Societies prioritize these two existential goals differently. Societies who score low on this dimension, for example, prefer to maintain time-honoured traditions and norms while viewing societal change with suspicion. Those with a culture which scores high, on the other hand, take a more pragmatic approach: they encourage thrift and efforts in modern education as a way to prepare for the future. In the business context this dimension is related to as "(short term) normative versus (long term) pragmatic" (PRA). In the academic environment the terminology Monumentalism versus Flexhumility is sometimes also used.
Indulgence versus Restraint (IND)	Indulgence stands for a society that allows relatively free gratification of basic and natural human drives related to enjoying life and having fun. Restraint stands for a society that suppresses gratification of needs and regulates it by means of strict social norms.

4   Methods and Results

Referring to the questionnaire we used in this study in Table 2, we measured all the key variables in our research model using 5-point scale with items adapted from Ma et al. (2015). Consumers' perception of the conversational function of the toy was measured by two items, "to what extent does the conversation function of Hello Barbie make sense to you" and "to what extent do you like the conversation function of Hello Barbie" ($r = 0.61$). Perceived risks of the conversational function of the toy was measured by three items, "I am afraid the conversation function including the recording function of Hello Barbie may violate the user's personal privacy/may gather too much of the user's information/may lead to some potential data security

Table 2 Questionnaire

No.	Question
1	Have you ever heard of or seen Hello Barbie before this talk?
2	Based on the information you received earlier, what was on your mind when you thought about the Hello Barbie? Please write a few lines to describe what came to your mind, such as its pros and cons.
3	How interested will you be in buying a Hello Barbie for yourself or a child?
4	What is the probability that you will buy a Hello Barbie for yourself or a child?
5	To what extent does the conversation function of Hello Barbie make sense to you?
6	To what extent do you like the conversation function of Hello Barbie?
7	Please evaluate how much you agree with the following statement: "Children between the age of 7 and 9 will enjoy playing with the Hello Barbie".
8	Please evaluate how much you agree with the following statement: "Children between the age of 10 and 13 will enjoy playing with the Hello Barbie".
9	I am afraid the conversation function including the recording function of Hello Barbie may violate the user's personal privacy.
10	I am worried that the conversation function including the recording function of Hello Barbie may gather too much of the user's information.
11	I am afraid that the conversation function including the recording function of Hello Barbie may lead to some potential data security issues in the future.
12	Do you perceive any other children safety issues with the Hello Barbie?
13	Please provide an overall evaluation of Hello Barbie after considering its benefits and potential risks.
14	Overall, what do you think of Hello Barbie?
15	How innovative do you think the Hello Barbie is?
16	I am usually among the first to try new products.
17	I like to buy new and different things.
18	What's your major (Graduate or Post-graduate)?
19	How long have you been using a smart phone (e.g., iPhone, Samsung Galaxy, etc.)?
20	Which operating system is running on your smart phone?
21	Have you ever tried any speech recognition app on your smart phone before? How often do you use this speech recognition app? Do you have any concern when using this speech recognition app?

issues in the future" (r = 0.89). Participants' perceived innovativeness of Hello Barbie was measured by one item, "how innovative do you think Hello Barbie is", ranging from "1 = not at all innovative" to "5 = very innovative." Consumers' attitude toward the Hello Barbie was measured by three items asking participants' overall evaluation of the toy being "very bad/very good," "very unfavorable/very favorable," and "not at all appealing/very appealing" (r = 0.82). Participants' overall evaluation of the toy considering its benefits and risks, ranging from "1 = risks outweigh benefits" to "5 = benefits outweigh risks." Participants' purchase intention toward the toy was measured by two items, "how interested will you be in buying a Hello Barbie for yourself or a child" and "what is the probability that you will buy a Hello Barbie for yourself or a child" (correlation r = 0.79). This study also measured participants' trait innovativeness, history of using smartphone and speech recognition software, whether they had heard of the toy before, and demographic variables as control variables.

One hundred and eighteen participants (73.9% male and 24.6% female) completed the questionnaire. Among them, forty-six (39%) were from Brazil and seventy-two (61%) were from Argentina. The average age was 28 years. We first analyzed whether Brazilian participants perceived Hello Barbie differently from Argentina participants. Analysis of Covariance (ANCOVA) with perception of the conversational function, perceived risks of the conversational function, perceived innovativeness, overall evaluation, attitudes and purchase intention as separate dependent variables and age, gender, number of children, whether they had seen the toy before, individual trait innovativeness, and speech recognition application usage as covariates shows that none of the covariates was significant. Therefore, these covariates were dropped in the analysis and we report the results of analysis of variance (ANOVA). As we have predicted, Brazilian participants perceived the conversational function of the toy better (3.54 vs. 2.95, $F(1, 116) = 8.41$, $p < 0.01$), had better overall evaluation given all the benefits and risks (2.93 vs. 2.15, $F(1, 116) = 16.25$, $p < 0.001$), had more positive attitudes toward the toy (3.25 vs. 2.57, $F(1, 116) = 14.24$, $p < 0.001$), and hence expressed higher purchase intention toward the toy (2.26 vs. 1.63, $F(1 116) = 14.17$, $p < 0.001$) than Argentina participants. However, different from our expectation, there was no significant difference between the Brazilian participants and Argentinian participants in their perceived risks of the conversational function (4.17 vs. 3.91, $F(1, 116) = 1.80$, $p > 0.1$) and perceived innovativeness of the toy (3.87 vs. 4.07, $F(1, 116) = 1.25$, $p > 0.2$). This result may suggest that the difference in uncertainty avoidance levels between the two countries has no impact on risk and innovativeness perception. We will explain this together with the results from the research model.

Second, we tested our proposed research model using structural equation modeling (Amos 24). The results are shown in Figs. 6 and 7. All the lines indicate significant relationships between variables. An interesting difference between the two models is that perceived innovativeness negatively affected people's overall evaluation of the toy in Argentina, but positively affected people's overall evaluation

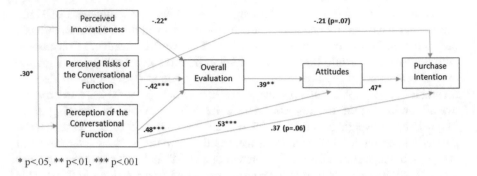

* p<.05, ** p<.01, *** p<.001

Fig. 6 Results in Argentina.

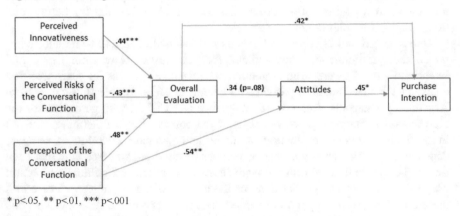

* p<.05, ** p<.01, *** p<.001

Fig. 7 Results in Brazil

of the toy in Brazil. In addition, in Argentina, the positive effect of the perceived innovativeness on overall evaluation is mediated by the perception of the conversational function. These results may suggest that uncertainty avoidance plays a more significant role in consumer new product adoption in Argentina than in Brazil. This may also help to explain our finding that there is no significant difference in perceived innovativeness and perceived risks between the two countries, which may suggest that uncertainty avoidance has no impact on risk perception and innovativeness perception. The two models show that although consumers in both countries may have similar levels of perceived innovativeness of the toy, Argentinian consumers perceive the newer the innovation the lower the evaluation, whereas Brazilian consumers perceived the newer the innovation the higher the evaluation, i.e., they prefer newer innovations. Brazilian consumers' preference for "newer" innovations finally lead to their higher purchase intention toward the toy.

5 Conclusion and Future Work

In summary, there are three properties of a smart toy: (1) Pervasive – a smart toy may follow child through everyday activities; (2) Social – social aspects and multiplayer are becoming a mandatory aspect of interactive smart toys in a one-to-one, one-to-many and many-to-many relations (Tath 2006); and (3) Connected – Smart toys may connect and communicate with other toys and services through networks. Children provide a unique user base which requires special attention in several key areas related to their privacy. Children's data is widely considered to be particularly sensitive and should be treated with extreme care by law and legislation (Toy Industry Association 2012). Privacy can result in physical safety of child user (McClary 2004). A framework is required which can achieve these privacy goals by minimizing the collection and retention of potentially sensitive user data, as well as involving the user (or parent) in the control of their child's data. End user requirements need to consider that the main user base is children, who have unique requirements as they are especially vulnerable and in order to protect their sensitive location data, parents/guardians require a method to implement privacy controls on their child's data. The results of our empirical study suggest that Hello Barbie can emphasize its innovativeness to enhance consumer acceptance in low uncertainty avoidance cultures such as Brazil. Whereas, in cultures with high uncertainty avoidance such as Argentina, Hello Barbie can reduced its perceived newness by associate it with existing technology such as voice recognition mobile apps to enhance consumers' evaluation of the toy. For future works, we are currently conducting this survey in Canada and Colombia in order to compare the difference between North America and South America in this emerging smart toy.

References

A&E Networks (2016) 1959 Barbie makes her debut, 26 November, 2016. Online: Available: http://www.history.com/this-day-in-history/barbie-makes-her-debut. Accessed 8 Feb 2017

Byrne C (2006) Hot toys are dead: long live hot products. Young Consum 7(1):8–13

Dudau V (2017) German agency tells parents to destroy smart toy due to fears it's being used to spy on kids, Neowin, 2017. Online: https://www.neowin.net/news/german-agency-tells-parents-to-destroy-smart-toy-due-to-fears-its-being-used-to-spy-on-kids. Accessed 18 Feb 2017

Goldstein J, Buckingham D, Brougère G (2004) Toys, games, and media, lawrence erlbaum associates. Publishers, Mahwah, New Jersey/London, p 262

Hains R (2014) 5 reasons NOT to buy barbie for little girls (it's not just body image!), 15 December, 2014. Online: Available: https://rebeccahains.com/2014/12/15/5-reasons-not-to-buy-barbie/. Accessed 8 Feb 2017

Hoeffler S (2003) Measuring preferences for really new products. J Mark Res 40(4):406–420

Hofstede G (2001) Culture's consequences: comparing values, behaviors, institutions, and organizations across nations, 2nd edn. Sage Publications, Thousand Oaks

Jhang JH, Grant SJ, Campbell MC, Campbell (2012) Get it? Got it. Good! Enhancing new product acceptance by facilitating resolution of extreme incongruity. J Mark Res 49:247–259

Ma Z, Gill T, Jiang Y (2015) Core versus peripheral innovations: the effect of innovation locus on consumer adoption of new products. J Mark Res 52(3):309–324

Mattel (2015) Hello barbie messaging Q&A, December 2015. Online: http://hellobarbiefaq.mattel.com/wp-content/uploads/2015/12/hellobarbie-faq-v3.pdf. Accessed 8 Feb 2017

McClary A (2004) Good toys, bad toys: how safety, society, politics and fashion have reshaped children's playthings. McFarland & Company, Jefferson, p 201

Michael K, Hayes A (2015) High-tech child's play in the cloud: be safe and aware of the difference between virtual and real. IEEE Consum Electron Mag 5(1):123–128

Moreau CP, Lehmann DR, Markman AB (2001) En-trenched knowledge structures and consumer response to new products. J of Mark Res 38(1):14–29

OEC (2017) The observatory of economic complexity, 2017. Online: http://atlas.media.mit.edu/en/. Accessed 17 Feb 2017

Tath EI (2006) Context data model for privacy. PRIME Standardization Workshop, p 1–6

Toy Industry Association (2012) The changing privacy and data security landscape – from mobile apps to OBA. Keller and Heckman LLP, Washington, D.C. Online: http://www.toyassociation.org/App_Themes/tia/pdfs/priorities/M2C/PrivacyWhitePaper.pdf

ToyTalk (2015) Speakalegend, 7 July, 2015. Online: https://www.toytalk.com/product/speakalegend/. Accessed 8 Feb 2017

Van den Bulte C, Stremersch S (2004) Social contagion and income heterogeneity in new product diffusion: a meta-analytic test. Mark Sci 23(4):530–544

Designing Hand Tracked Exergames with Virtual Toys

Saskia Ortiz-Padilla, Alvaro Uribe-Quevedo, and Bill Kapralos

1   Introduction

The interest in Virtual Reality (VR) has been recently renewed given the current availability of consumer-level hardware, thus providing the possibility of mass-impacting various industries (e.g., entertainment, tourism, education, advertisement, maintenance, medicine, health care and training amongst many others) (Kamel Boulos et al. 2017). Traditionally, VR hardware and software was cost-prohibitive and targeted towards industrial and research centers. However, the landscape is changing thanks to the advances and research in the videogame industry aimed at providing newer forms of immersion and interaction. VR headsets such as, the Occulus Rift, HTC Vive, and mobile phone-based VR, are taking the lead (Table 1 presents a comparison of traditional and current VR head-mounted displays).

One of the primary challenges of VR relates to interactions with the real word, particularly through the sense of touch. Numerous user interfaces have been designed to include the sense of touch, from exoskeletons (e.g., CyberGrasp) (Nikolakis et al. 2004), haptics (e.g., Novint Falcon) (Martin and Hillier 2009), to rumble controllers (e.g., Wiimote controller) (Lee 2008), and motion capture (e.g., Kinect V2) (Xu and McGorry 2015). User input interfaces have also gone from cost-prohibitive devices to consumer-level solutions involving motion tracking through

S. Ortiz-Padilla • A. Uribe-Quevedo (✉)
Universidad Militar Nueva Granada, Bogota, Colombia
e-mail: saskiaortiz44@gmail.com; alvaro.j.uribe@ieee.org

B. Kapralos
University of Ontario Institute of Technology, Oshawa, ON, Canada
e-mail: bill.kapralos@uoit.ca

© Springer International Publishing AG 2017
J.K.T. Tang, P.C.K. Hung (eds.), *Computing in Smart Toys*, International Series on Computer Entertainment and Media Technology,
DOI 10.1007/978-3-319-62072-5_4

Table 1 Comparison of traditional VR and modern VR headsets (information obtained from the website of each manufacturer)

Device	Year	Resolution	Horizontal field of view	Price (USD)
Cybermind vissette	2005	1280 × 1024	36°	<$10,000
i-Glasses	2005	800 × 600	26°	<$1,200
Proview XL	1998	1024 × 768	40°	$15,000
nVisor ST50	2003	1280 × 1024	40°	$19,700
Oculus VR	2016	1200 × 180	110°	$599
HTC VIVE	2016	1200 × 1080	110°	$799
Google Daydream	2016	1440 × 1280	Phone dependent	$79
Google Cardboard	2014	Phone dependent	Phone dependent	$10
Mattel's Viewmaster	2015	Phone dependent	98°	$30

Table 2 Comparison of 3D user interfaces (Information obtained from the website of each manufacturer)

Device	Force feedback	Degrees of freedom	Price (USD)
Cybergrasp	12 N per finger	22	~$80,0000
Quanser's HD2	19.71 N (X), 19.71 N (Y), 13.94 N (Z)	6	~$60,000–70,000
Geomagic Touch	3.3 N	5	$2,000
Novint Falcon	8.9 N	3	$250
3D Touch	3.3 N	5	$600
Kinect	NA	20 joint tracking	Discontinued
Kinect V2	NA	25 joint tracking	$100
Leap Motion	NA	22 joint tracking	$70

inertial measuring units (IMUs) (Lee 2008), and image processing (Lachat et al. 2015). Table 2 presents a comparison of 3D user interfaces with and without haptics feedback.

The exposure to innovative technological tools is changing how we interact with the world with the internet and mobile phones reshaping our lives (Colbert et al. 2016). However, excessive exposure or improper use of any information and communication technologies (ICT) (e.g., smartphone, handheld video game consoles, tablets, laptops, etc.), increases the risk of acquiring musculoskeletal diseases resulting from bad posture, repetitive movements, or prolonged seating (Gustafsson et al. 2017; Luttmann et al. 2016). Prior to the mass installment of ICT globally, the majority of musculoskeletal problems occurred "on the job" during regular working hours. However, this has changed with the proliferation of ICT and mobile devices. Now, musculoskeletal problems, particularly those related to the use of personal computing devices, have greatly increased thus impacting and often times, negatively affecting affect quality of life (Kee et al. 2016).

The primary strategy to prevent and reduce the risk of developing a musculoskeletal disorder is physical activity/exercise and proper use of personal computing/technological devices. Common methods used to promote physical activity include printed guides, multimedia tools, demonstrations, and most recently, video games (Cornick and Blascovich 2017; Knights et al. 2014). In a manner similar, to physical toys, virtual toys require interactions through user interfaces that can result in musculoskeletal disorders (Yap and Paul 2017). The belief of the sedentary gamer changed since the launch of the Nintendo Wii in 2006. The Nintendo Wii is a video game console that included the Wii Remote controller, which detects movement in three dimensions allowing it to be used as a handheld pointing device thus permitting for novel game interactions (Wingrave et al. 2010). From this point, given the immense popularity of the Nintendo Wii, and the Wii remote controller in particular, other game console manufacturers began examining motion-based interactions to create novel, compelling, and immersive experiences, and this spawned numerous body-tracked games for all ages (e.g., Microsoft's Kinect and the PlayStation Move) (Neufeldt 2009). Given the ability to track the body (or parts of it), physical activity was a key component of many of these games. The coupling of gaming and exercise, whereby playing a video game becomes a form of physical activity, is known as exergaming (Sinclair et al. 2007). Exergames take advantage of the engaging, interactive, and fun inherent in video games to promote physical activity, and promote engagement with training or rehabilitation (Smith and Schoene 2012), which can be mundane and repetitive (Kato 2010). When compared to traditional exercise, exergaming has been linked to greater frequency and intensity of physical activity and enhanced health outcomes (Annesi and Mazas 1997). Although many exergames have been developed for mainstream consoles (e.g., Your Shape: Fitness Evolved, Dance Dance Revolution, and Wii Sports, amongst many others), it is within the realm of health care that exergames are most successful (Peng et al. 2011).

Exergaming in healthcare has produced diverse solutions that address patient conditions related to stroke, physiotherapy, physical activity in the elderly (Kato 2010), With respect to hand musculoskeletal disorders, it is common to find that patients suffering from the carpal tunnel syndrome, tendinitis and tenosynovitis, could have prevented their condition by exercising and improving working habits (Pätiälä et al. 1985). In most cases, the condition goes undiagnosed because the person doesn't manifest any discomfort to the physician, and even when detected, the assessment is subjective, conducted through observation and self-reported progression from the patient (Tang et al. 2015). Another factor that affects health care exercises (whether from prevention, rehabilitation, or maintenance), is that such type of exercises require extensive repetition that can become boring, particularly with a lack of feedback when self-conducted (Burdea 2002).

According to the World Health Organization's Preventing Musculoskeletal Disorders book (Luttmann et al. 2016), it is important to exercise and improve working habits. One body member that plays an important role in our daily interactions is the human hand, which allows us to execute precision and power grasping tasks (Dragulescu et al. 2007). Hand-based interactions have taken a bigger role in computer and other systems (e.g., touch and gestures), as they provide means to facilitate taking advantage of the working space of the upper limb (Hneineh et al. 2016). In this chapter, we present the design of an exergame that employs virtual toys whose interactions are purposely developed to rely on hand exercises. Our goal is to develop an engaging scenario that motivates the exertion of hand movements that will aid in strengthing the hand and (ideally) limit injury while playing a game with a consumer-level device.

2 The Design and Development Process

In this section, we present the design and development methods employed to develop the exergame with virtual toys through the use of hand tracking. To develop the exergame, we approached the problem by analyzing the hand, its movements, conditions, and exercises. This allowed us to identify the system's inputs and outputs, and to determine the game interactions based on the desired hand motions. After defining the game elements, we choose the appropriate consumer-level tools and implement the games.

2.1 About the Human Hand

The human hand is comprised of bones, ligaments, tendons and muscles, all of which provide dexterity to conduct several grasping and precision actions (Dragulescu et al. 2007). The prehensile tasks can be performed by flexion of the fingers, which are comprised by a proximal, medial and distal phalanx, with two degrees of freedom (DOF) at the base of the palm, and one DOF between the medial and distal phalanx. However, the thumb behaves differently as the proximal phalanx moves with the metacarpal bone to provide a rotation that allows it to oppose the other fingers. Figure 1 presents the bones and DOF of the hand, while the hand's range of movements is provided in Table 3.

Fig. 1 Bones and degrees of freedom of the human hand

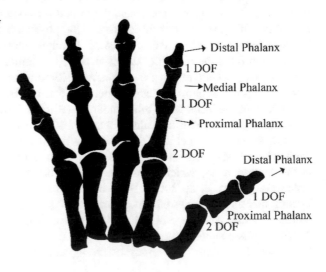

Table 3 Finger's rotational ranges

Joint	Standard rotation
Proximal	90°
Medial	110°
Distal	60–70°

Table 4 Musculoskeletal disorders of the hand

MD	Description
Tunnel Carpal Syndrome	It occurs when the median nerve that goes from the forearm to the hand is pressured within the tunnel. Depending on the stage the treatment involves medication, therapy, or surgery.
Tendinitis	Tendon joint inflammation caused by an injury. Treatment involves rest, therapy, medication or surgery.
Tenosynovitis	Inflammation of the tissue surrounding the tendons. It can be caused by overloading forces or an infection. The treatment involves rest, medication or surgery.

2.1.1 Musculoskeletal Hand Disorders

Musculoskeletal disorders (MD) affect the locomotor apparatus (i.e., muscles tendons, cartilage, ligaments, and nerves). The severity of the disorders can range from light, transitory, irreversible, or disabling (Luttmann et al. 2016). One main cause of developing musculoskeletal disorders is associated with repetitive activities that, when poorly performed, can lead to health risks. Amongst the body segments with most common MDs are the back and the upper limb. In this chapter, we focus on the hand as part of the upper limb that can suffer from carpal tunnel syndrome, tendinitis, tenosynovitis, and arthritis. Causes of MDs on the hand include: (i) typing, (ii) handheld operations, (iii) prolonged vibrations, (iv) other repetitive movements (Barr et al. 2004). Table 4 presents a summary of some of the musculoskeletal disorders of the hand, their description, and common treatments.

2.1.2 Exercise and Physiotherapy

To keep the hand fully functional and in good health, exercise is recommended as it helps prevent and reduce the risk of MDs (Luttmann et al. 2016). Depending on the level of the disorder, a patient will go through two types of treatment: (i) preventive (e.g., routine and occupational health exercises), and (ii) post-operative (e.g., wound treatment, scar control, inflammatory reduction, pain management), to incorporate the patient back to normal life and work. Traditionally, the exercise routines were provided in the form of printed guides, demonstration, and oral descriptions of what the patient is required to do. In some cases, depending on the severity of the condition, the patient attends a health care facility where guided routines are provided. However, exercising often becomes a challenging task as it depends on several factors including: (i) the patient's motivation (affected by the patient's will

Table 5 Basic hand exercises (5 Exercises to improve hand mobility, Harvard Medical School. http://www.health.harvard.edu/pain/5-exercises-to-improve-hand-mobility-and-reduce-pain. Accessed on April 2017)

Exercise	Visual representation
Flexion/extension	
Abduction/adduction	
Prehensile	

to recover, and pain), (ii) an understanding of the exercises and the condition with its associated risks, (iii) lack of time, and (iv) lack of feedback (Burdea 2002).

One area of focus for the prevention of MDs is preventive exercising and this often involves a routine series of movements performed during working hours to relax the tendons and strengthen the muscles. The most basic exercise includes movements of flexion/extension (rotating the hand up and down relative to the upper arm), abduction/adduction (rotating the hand in and out away from the forearm), and prehensile movements that involve opening and closing the fingers as if securing an object within the hand. Table 5 provides a graphical illustration of how to properly perform the aforementioned exercises.

It is worth noting that there are other exercises that can be performed with a combination of the movements presented in Table 5 (see. Fig. 2 for a graphical illustration of these exercises):

(a) Neutral wrist with extended fingers and thumb
(b) Fist connector
(c) Fist flexion
(d) Extended forearm, palm, and flexed fingers

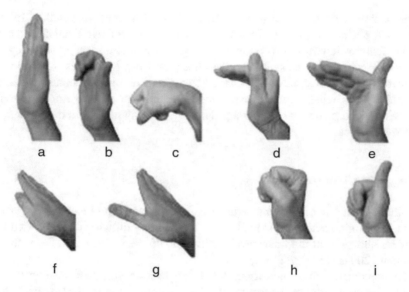

Fig. 2 Combinatory exercises (5 Exercises to improve hand mobility, Harvard Medical School. http://www.health.harvard.edu/pain/5-exercises-to-improve-hand-mobility-and-reduce-pain. Accessed on April 2017)

(e) Hand as table
(f) Straight palm
(g) Straight palm with extended thumb
(h) Fist with extended thumb

To properly execute these exercises, it is important to consider two key aspects: (i) matching the postures as close as possible, and (ii) performing the exercises at regular intervals (the literature suggests every hour for approximately 5 minutes) (Rozmaryn et al. 1998).

2.2   Tracking Technology

With a basic understanding of the hand and its range of motions, we can now choose the most suitable technology for the hand-based exergame. To avoid causing any discomfort by wearing any external devices or alter the natural movements of the hand, we aim to choose a non-invasive consumer-level 3D user interface that allows for natural movements. During our research, we discovered several hand-based user interfaces that require the user to wear a glove (e.g., 5DT glove, the Peregrine glove, and the Human glove), which introduces additional costs in addition to hygiene, maintenance, and mass adoption issues. We then turned to vision-based solutions, particularly those that have become mass-market products through consumer-level devices. Two devices, in particular, the Leap Motion (Smeragliuolo et al. 2016), and Microsoft's Kinect version 2 (Xu and McGorry 2015) stood out. Each device offers unique features in terms of working area, sensor resolution, tracking accuracy, and integration with other technologies. We chose the Leap Motion as it is becoming standard (built-in) with newer laptops[1], keyboards[2], and head mounted displays[3], and this can provide a mobile experience that doesn't require external devices such as a video game console, gamepads, and a display/monitor required with the Microsoft Kinect.

2.2.1 Hand Tracking Setup

To start with the hand tracking setup, we first analyzed the Leap Motion sensor. The Leap Motion achieves 3D tracking of the hand by utilizing three infrared light emitters and two infrared cameras within a 60.96 cm^2 area and a field of view between 120 and 150 (see Fig. 3).

To implement hand interactions the Leap Motion software development kit (SDK) allows calculating the fingers, hand and forearm position based on the depth information provided by the infrared cameras. Finger position and orientation can

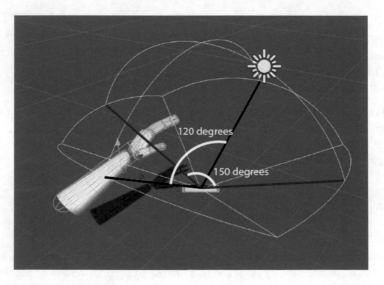

Fig. 3 Leap Motion tracking area

---

[1]Leap Motion Laptop, http://www8.hp.com/us/en/ads/envy-leap-motion/overview.html?jumpid=va_r11260_go_leapmotion. Accessed on April 2017

[2]Leap Motion keyboard, https://support.hp.com/us-en/product/Keyboards/6875294/model/6875306/drivers. Accessed on April 2017

[3]Mobile VR, https://www.leapmotion.com/product/vr#110, Accessed on April 2017

be determined if the cameras have a direct line of sight of the fingertips. When occluded, the inverse kinematics estimation can be easily lost either by the position of the hand when the fingers are not visible or in certain lighting conditions that may affect the infrared cameras. Another initialization/setup parameter to consider is the distance between the hands and the sensor since the tracking environment must be configured in a manner that guarantees proper data collection. The first consideration is that the hand must hover above approximately 15 cm above the sensor.

2.2.2 Hand Exercises Implementation

To implement the hand exercises, we defined the motion ranges based on occupational health care guides[4] with the following characteristics:

(a) Flexion/Extension: Maximum downward rotation of 90° and minimum configurable rotation set by default to 60°.
(b) Abduction: Maximum rotation towards the little finger is approximately 30°, with minimum configurable ration set by default to 10°.
(c) Adduction: Maximum rotation towards the thumb of approximately 20°, with minimum configurable ration set by default to 10°.
(d) Prehensile: Full flexed fingers, maximum rotation of 100°, with minimum configurable ration set by default to 80°.

The movements described above are presented graphically in Fig. 4.

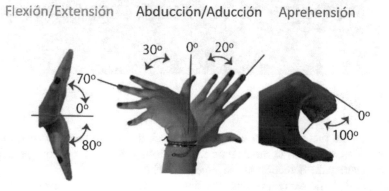

Fig. 4 Flexion/extension, abduction/adduction, and prehensile ranges of movement

---

[4]5 Exercises to improve hand mobility, Harvard Medical School. http://www.health.harvard.edu/pain/5-exercises-to-improve-hand-mobility-and-reduce-pain. Accessed on April 2017.

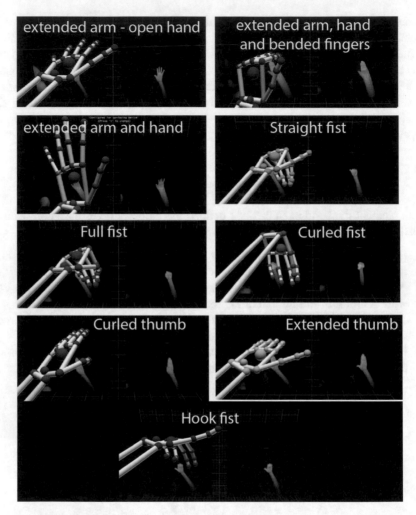

Fig. 5 Leap Motion hand tracking validation

To validate that the sensor can properly track the desired movements, the Leap Motion SDK was used to run a demo while printing the joint rotations presented in Fig. 2 to verify the detection of movements as shown in Fig. 5.

To develop the exergame with the hand exercise data, we chose the Unity3D game engine and the Leap Motion SDK, as these tools allow cross-platform development and compatibility with other VR hardware (e.g., Oculus Rift, HTC Vive). Since the games will involve visual feedback, we chose the Blender3D open source graphics platform to develop all of the 3D computer graphics content.

2.3   Game Design

The game design process includes various stages: (i) defining the game elements, (ii) defining inputs and outputs, and finally, (iii) defining the system architecture. We began by defining the goal of our game modules, which is to provide and engaging form of exercising through virtual toys interactions. To achieve this goal, we set to design three games associated with the movements presented in Table 5.

2.3.1   Module 1: Extension/Flexion

The first module of the exergame presents a lake in the middle of a forest where a family of ducks lives. The main character is a duckling who lost his family and must find them within a specific time frame. The game elements are defined as presented in Table 6.

The inputs to the game are the flexion and extension movements of each hand and the ranges are defined on the exercises presented in Fig. 4. The motion of each hand is mapped to each of the duckling's legs that serve as propellers while swimming.

Table 6 Game 1 elements

Player	Single player with interactions based on hand tracking flexion/extension.
Process	Flexion and extension movements mapped to the duckling's legs to swim through the lake.
Objectives	Reach the goal by collecting all the scattered coins throughout the lake before 80 s.
Rules	The duck swims as the result of the flexion/extension movements. Direction can be changed by moving either one of the hands. Reaching the goal within the allocated time frame. A coin is collected when the duck goes through it. Reaching the goal triggers the end of the game (and the end of the game screen is displayed). When the time elapses, the game ends (and the end of game screen is displayed) Bad hand movements impede swimming. Reaching the checkpoints provide additional time.
Resources	Coins: Provide a scoring mechanism that allows beating personal records. Time: Diminishing resource starting at 80 s. Additional time (20 s) can be added by going through the checkpoints. The visualization of the duck's legs provides the player with feedback, allowing the player to determine whether the movements are being properly performed.
Conflict	Time-constraint; when the allotted time has elapsed, the game is over and restarted.
Limits	Lake boundaries.
Outcome	The game ends when the player gathers all the coins within the specified time frame or when the time elapses.

Table 7 Game 2 elements

Player	Single player with interactions based on hand tracking abduction/adduction.
Process	Adduction/abduction movements are mapped to the frog's legs to swim through the swamp.
Objectives	Reach the goal by collecting all of the scattered food throughout the swamp before the allocated time of 80 s elapses.
Rules	The frog swims as the result of the abduction/adduction movements. Direction can be changed by moving either one of the hands. Reaching the goal within the allocated time frame. Food collection occurs when the duck goes through each food item. Reaching the goal signifies the end of the game and the end of the game screen is displayed. When the elapses, the game ends and the end of the game screen is displayed. Bad hand movements impede swimming. Reaching the checkpoints provide additional time (20 s).
Resources	Food: Provides a scoring mechanism that allows beating personal records. Time: Diminishing resource starting with 80 s. Additional time (20 s) can be added by going through the checkpoints. The visualization of the frog's legs provides the player with feedback, allowing them to observe whether their movements being properly performed.
Conflict	Time-constraint, when the allotted time has elapsed, the game is over and restarted.
Limits	Lake boundaries.
Outcome	The game ends when the player gathers all the coins within the specified time or when the time has elapsed.

2.3.2 Module 2: Abduction/Adduction

The second module of the exergame presents a swamp in the middle of the forest where a family of flies lurks around the waste. The main character is a starving frog who must find food before it is too late. The game elements are presented in Table 7.

The inputs of the game are the abduction and adduction movements, with the ranges defined as presented in Fig. 4. The motion of each hand is mapped to each of the frog's legs that serve as propellers while swimming. The 3D character was modelled and rigged in Blender 3D and other virtual elements such as the flies, goal, and terrain were modeled after real-life counterparts to have a consistent look in the game.

2.3.3 Module 3: Grasp/Prehensile Tasks

The third and final module of the exergame takes place in a chemical laboratory where the player is the laboratory technician in charge of disposing of the hazardous materials to avoid a nuclear catastrophe. The player has 160 s to organize the labeled materials by grabbing them and securely placing them in target areas. The game elements are presented in Table 8.

Table 8 Game 3 elements

Player	Single player with interactions based on hand tracking abduction/adduction.
Process	Prehensile movements mapped to grab the chemicals.
Objectives	Reach the goal by collecting all of the chemicals scattered throughout the laboratory before the 160 s allotted time elapses.
Rules	The chemicals labeled with the letter R have to be grabbed and deposited only using the right hand without releasing them. The chemicals labeled with the letter L have to be grabbed and deposited only using the left hand without releasing them. Chemicals only disappear if placed in the proper container according to their colors. The game is completed when all chemicals have been properly deposited. Complete the game before the time elapses. When the time elapses, the game is over
Resources	Score Mechanism: 20 points for each properly disposed of the chemical. Score allows beating personal records Time: Diminishing resource starting with 80 s. Additional time (20 s) can be added by going through the checkpoints. Visualization of the virtual hand provides the player with feedback, allowing them to determine whether movements are being properly done.
Conflict	When the allocated time has elapsed, the game ends and must be restarted.
Limits	Laboratory walls
Outcome	The game ends when the player properly deposits the chemicals within the allotted time.

2.4 System Architecture

With the hand, exercise, and game design information, we defined a system architecture that allows an iterative and flexible approach to develop the hand exergame and its three modules. The system is configured to receive user inputs in the form of mouse and keyboard interactions, to setup basic profile information, and when in the game, the interactions are based on the hand movements that the user is required to perform. The graphical user interface (GUI) inputs are programmed in a manager script. In-game interactions are also programmed in a script that defines the motion ranges and suitable tracking area. This information is processed by the Unity scene, whose scripts react to the user inputs. The outputs provide visual and audio feedback from the game interactions. Additionally, a report is created after each game is played so the user is aware of the progress with each exergame. The subsystems of the architecture provide solutions for managing user data, exergame configurations, and to report data for further assessment by a health care specialist. The system architecture is presented in Fig. 6.

2.5 Graphical User Interface (GUI)

The three modules of the exergame are under one Main menu with a tree branching structure. Each game provides the following menus: (i) play, (ii) instructions, (iii)

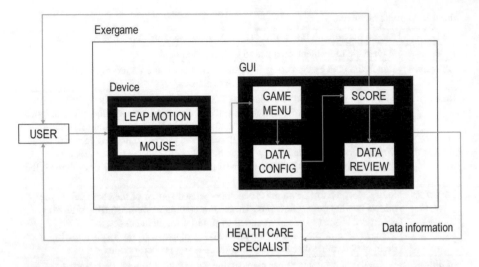

Fig. 6 System architecture

Fig. 7 In-game menus

about, and (iv) exit. Since the games require a maximum of two minutes to be completed, no pause option is included in either of the exergames. The in-game menus are presented in Fig. 7.

3 Results

In this section, we present preliminary results obtained from implementation and validation on the hand exergames. Figure 8 presents the scenarios for each exergame.

After each game is completed, the system provides feedback regarding player performance during the game. The rotation and prehensile data is saved in a plain text file and displays the score and the average rotation angles for all exercises (Fig. 9).

3.1 Validation

To validate each of the modules of the hand exergame, we invited participants to try them and provide feedback. Two main configurations were employed during the games. In the first configuration, the player plays with the arms extended over the Leap Motion on all three modules, while in the second configuration, the arms rested on a cushion to avoid the discomfort of sustaining them in the air. A graphical illustration of both configurations is provided in Fig. 10. The need for the cushion

Fig. 8 Scenarios for each module of the exergame (Duck, Frog, and Laboratory Technician)

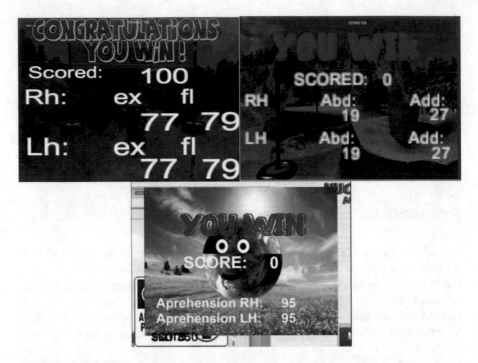

Fig. 9 End-game feedback

Fig. 10 Exergame hand tracking setup (with and without cushion)

was the result of a preliminary survey conducted with 10 participants between the ages of 22 and 26, each working with computers for approximately 40 h per week. During the gameplay sessions, participants received instructions regarding how to complete the game, and after playing each module once, they expressed the discomfort of having their arms extended over the sensor for the durations of games (a minimum of 80 s and a maximum of 160 s). After trying the three modules, all participants expressed interest in doing more exergaming with hand-based motion tracking. Participants also expressed interest in the novelty of the Leap Motion and were not aware of its inclusion on laptops and keyboards, or as a standalone device During each participant interactions, we observed usability improvements to be implemented in terms of adjusting the ranges of interaction (using a calibration scene for each module prior it begins), and clearer user feedback to keep the players engaged.

Finally, we invited 15 different participants to experiment with the modified and improved versions of the exergames within the same age ranges and and also work with computers for approximately 40 h each week. In this case, we included a calibration tool to adjust the maximum and minimum ranges of motion that also allowed to identify possible tracking errors due to clothing (e.g., wearing gloves) or lighting. As in the previous exploration, participants were asked to navigate through the modules, explore, and complete them. After the exergaming experience, participants completed a survey that provided the following insight: All agreed that the most difficult module to complete was Module 2; during our observation and debriefing period, we observed that abduction and adduction rotations were challenging, particularly given the lack of practice. All participants agreed that the gaming components made them forget about exercising and reoriented their attention to the competition and completion aspects of the game. 71% agreed on the potential of exergames for engaging in hand exercising, while the rest expressed concern regarding users not liking the technology. 50% found the interactions suitable, the rest expressed having motion tracking difficulties which affected the gaming flow while playing, and finally, all expressed interest in using the exergames instead of traditional exercise tools.

4 Discussion

In this chapter, we have presented three hand-based exergames using interactions with virtual toys whose actions are controlled by the user's hand movements. Based on our preliminary results, the interactions and game elements are capable of distracting users from what is typically considered boring hand exercises, by shifting their attention to their score and reaching the goal. Despite the low-cost of the Leap Motion and its availability in laptops and keyboards, clothing and lighting can create unfavorable conditions that can affect the gaming experience. This is particularly critical since it can draw users away from the game. Accounting for lighting conditions is a challenging topic due to hardware limitations, even though the Leap Motion manufacturers are working on software improvements to enhance accuracy and tracking.

One interesting behavior observed during the gameplay was that several participants tried to reach the goal by moving their hands faster, only to discover that rapid movements were not being properly detected. The chosen time and pace for the exergames was based upon occupational health care recommendation from an expert, hence users are encouraged to focus on proper movements rather than rapid versions of them. After comparing all rotational data from the exercises, we observed that all users were within the set thresholds, showing that users followed the movements as expected.

Finally, we conclude that the potential of exergames, combined with consumer-level technologies, can provide a mass market solution to address health care challenges with exercises that are traditionally seen as an obligation, rather than a vital activity to prevent musculoskeletal disorders.

4.1 Future Work

Future work will focus on the development of more content providing virtual interactions with a different type of elements including toys. The potential of exergames can impact users and content plays an important role to reach multiple audiences. Since social media is currently driving users, we will seek to study how leaderboards and sharing exercise performance can impact the exergaming. Additionally, other aspects of toy computing will be pursued in terms of security, privacy, and safety. Future work will also include more formal effectiveness testing through the use of pre- and post-testing.

References

Annesi JJ, Mazas J (1997) Effects of virtual reality-enhanced exercise equipment on adherence and exercise-induced feeling states. Percept Mot Skills 85(3):835–844

Barr AE, Barbe MF, Clark BD (2004) Work-related musculoskeletal disorders of the hand and wrist: epidemiology, pathophysiology, and sensorimotor changes. J Orthop Sports Phys Ther 34(10):610–627

Burdea G (2002) Key note address: virtual rehabilitation-benefits and challenges. 1st International Workshop on Virtual Reality Rehabilitation (Mental Health, Neurological, Physical, Vocational) VRMHR 2002, Piscataway

Colbert A, Yee N, George G (2016) The digital workforce and the workplace of the future. Acad Manag J 59(3):731–739. Retrieved from http://amj.aom.org/content/59/3/731.short

Cornick J, Blascovich J (2017) Physiological responses to virtual exergame feedback for individuals with different levels of exercise self-efficacy. Int J Virtual Real 17(1):32–53

Dragulescu D, Perdereau V, Drouin M, Ungureanu L, Menyhardt K (2007) 3D active workspace of human hand anatomical model. Biomed Eng Online 6:15

Gustafsson E, Thomée S, Grimby-Ekman A (2017) Texting on mobile phones and musculoskeletal disorders in young adults: a five-year cohort study. Appl Ergon 58:208–214

Hneineh HN, Moselmani AA, Hage-Diab A, Saleh S (2016) Impaired hand movement tracking device with real-time visual feedback. In Biomedical Engineering (MECBME), 2016 3rd Middle East Conference on (pp. 72–75). IEEE, Beirut

Kato PM (2010) Video games in health care: closing the gap. Rev Gen Psychol 14(2):113

Kamel Boulos MN, Lu Z, Guerrero P, Jennett C, Steed A (2017) From urban planning and emergency training to Pokémon Go: applications of virtual reality GIS (VRGIS) and augmented reality GIS (ARGIS) in personal, public and environmental health. Int J Health Geogr 16(7):11

Kee I, Byun J, Jung J, Choi J (2016) The presence of altered craniocervical posture and mobility in smartphone-addicted teenagers with temporomandibular disorders. J Phys Ther Sci 28(2):339–346

Knights S, Graham N, Switzer L, Hernandez H, Ye Z, Findlay B, Xie WY, Wright V, Fehlings D (2014) An innovative cycling exergame to promote cardiovascular fitness in youth with cerebral palsy: a brief report. Dev Neurorehabil 19(2):1–6

Lachat E, Macher H, Mittet M-A, Landes T, Grussenmeyer P (2015) First experiences with kinect V2 sensor for close range 3D modelling. Int Arch Photogramm Remote Sens Spat Inf Sci. Suppl XL(5):93–100

Lee JC (2008) Hacking the nintendo Wii remote. IEEE Pervasive Comput 7:39–45

Luttmann A, Jäger M, Griefahn B (2016) Protecting workers' health series no. 5, preventing musculoskeletal disorders in the workplace, 2003. World Health Organization, Berlin

Martin S, Hillier N (2009) Characterisation of the Novint Falcon haptic device for application as a robot manipulator. Australasian Conference on Robotics and Automation, Sydney, p 291–292

Neufeldt C (2009) Wii play with elderly people. Interaction Spaces by Social Media for the Elderly, Bonn 6(3):50–59.

Nikolakis G, Tzovaras D, Moustakidis S, Strintzis MG (2004) CyberGrasp and PHANTOM integration: enhanced haptic access for visually impaired users. In: SPECOM'2004: 9th conference speech and computer, St. Petersburg, pp x1–x7

Pätiälä H, Rokkanen P, Kruuna O, Taponen E, Toivola M, Häkkinen V (1985) Carpal tunnel syndrome. Arch Orthop Trauma Surg 104(2):69–73

Peng W, Lin J, Crouse J (2011) Is playing exergames really exercising? A meta-analysis of energy expenditure in active video games. Cyberpsychol Behav Soc Netw 14(11):681–688

Rozmaryn LM, Dovelle S, Rothman ER, Gorman K, Olvey KM, Bartko JJ (1998) Nerve and tendon gliding exercises and the conservative management of carpal tunnel syndrome. J Hand Ther 11(3):171–179

Sinclair J, Hingston P, Masek M (2007) Considerations for the design of exergames. In: Proceedings of the 5th international conference on computer graphics and interactive techniques in Australia and Southeast Asia, pp 289–295

Smeragliuolo AH, Hill NJ, Disla L, Putrino D (2016) Validation of the leap motion controller using markered motion capture technology. J Biomech 49(9):1742–1750

Smith ST, Schoene D (2012) The use of exercise-based videogames for training and rehabilitation of physical function in older adults: current practice and guidelines for future research. Aging Health 8(3):243–252

Tang R, Yang X-D, Bateman S, Jorge J, Tang A (2015) Physio@home exploring visual guidance and feedback techniques for physiotherapy exercises. In: Proceedings of the 33rd annual ACM conference on human factors in computing systems - CHI '15. ACM Press, New York, pp 4123–4132

Wingrave CA, Williamson B, Varcholik PD, Rose J, Miller A, Charbonneau E, Bott J, JJ LV Jr (2010) The Wiimote and beyond: spatially convenient devices for 3D user interfaces. IEEE Comput Graph Appl 30:71–85

Xu X, McGorry RW (2015) The validity of the first and second generation Microsoft Kinect™ for identifying joint center locations during static postures. Appl Ergon 49:47

Yap S-S, Paul G (2017) Video gaming and its implications on the epidemiology of office work related upper limb disorders. In: Advances in social & occupational ergonomics. Springer, Cham, pp 201–213

Robot Toys for Children with Disabilities

Carlos T. Valadão, Silas F. R. Alves, Christiane M. Goulart,
and Teodiano F. Bastos-Filho

1 Introduction

The act of playing provides a positive contribution in the development of intellectual, social, psychological, motor, sensory-perceptual functions, being a means for entertainment and that can more effectively engage children and teenagers with disabilities in structured and protracted rehabilitation therapies (Hsieh 2008; Wu et al. 2012). Toys can trigger well-being in children, contribute for their physical, mental and social development, help them to deal with experience and reality and enable they to demonstrate and express their emotional needs in a developmentally appropriate way (Ray et al. 2013; Fontes et al. 2010). Therefore, toys can be employed as tools in alternative therapies to soften behavioural and psychological symptoms of stress experiences and disorders, as dementia, for instance. In this case, therapies using dolls have been fostered as a strategy in managing challenging behaviours in people with dementia, for example helping them to deal with attachment behaviour possibly present at various stages, besides reducing agitation, aggression and other behavioural patterns common to this disorder (Fernandez et al. 2013).

Therapeutic toys are able to provide physical and emotional welfare in children, mitigating their experiences in a situation of hospitalization (Fontes et al. 2010;

C.T. Valadão • C.M. Goulart • T.F. Bastos-Filho
Assistive Technology Centre, Federal University of Espirito Santo, Av. Fernando Ferrari, 514, 29075-910, Vitória, ES, Brazil
e-mail: carlos.valadao@ufes.br; christiane.ufes@gmail.com; teodiano.bastos@ufes.br

S.F.R. Alves (✉)
Mechanical and Industrial Engineering Department, University of Toronto, 5 King's College Road, M5S 3G8, Toronto, ON, Canada
e-mail: silas.alves@gmail.com; silas.alves@utoronto.ca

© Springer International Publishing AG 2017
J.K.T. Tang, P.C.K. Hung (eds.), *Computing in Smart Toys*, International Series on Computer Entertainment and Media Technology,
DOI 10.1007/978-3-319-62072-5_5

Sposito et al. 2016). Thus, these toys may be classified as ordinary, i.e. play materials that parents and children can purchase from toy shops; or adaptive, i.e. play materials that have been modified for different needs or treatment goals of children with developmental disabilities (Hsieh 2008). In addition, they allow children to express their feelings, facilitating the identification of their afflictions by professionals, prepare them for hospitalization and contribute to their physical improvement (Fontes et al. 2010). One example is a ludic setting where appropriate surgical and curative materials and hospital clothes are placed on dolls to prepare children for surgeries (Fontes et al. 2010), reducing possible negative feelings and thoughts.

In order to enhance the verbal communication and the closeness between children and health professionals, strategies as toys, pictures, drawings, storytelling and dramatizations may be beneficial to the understanding of the children's feelings, reactions and opinions. According to children's cognitive, emotional and physical development, finger puppets can be a playful means for increasing interaction and communication with children with cancer in hospital environment, aiding therapeutic purposes allied to the reduction of children's anxiety and fear, teaching tactics to promote healthy and exploration of the children's knowledge about their disease (Sposito et al. 2016).

Taking into account the technological advances in the field of infant-juvenile games and toys for entertainment and also therapeutic purposes, virtual reality games and robots have been becoming increasingly present in the routine of children and adolescents, especially of those have any cognitive, behavioural or motor disorder. Researchers highlight the effectiveness of technologies based on virtual reality as support to the therapeutic games, due to the capability of facilitating learning, enhancing attentional control, besides generating greater cognitive flexibility, perception, task switching and better address developmental disorders (Komendziński et al. 2016). These games and toys are an important and stimulant alternative or a complement to traditional therapies for children and adolescents with movement difficulties, once these therapies tend to be repetitive and grant scarce stimuli to keep children and adolescents' minds occupied (Wuang et al. 2011).

Depending on the nature of the disability or the invariable intervention setting, infant-juvenile individuals might show difficulty in repeated practice of functional tasks (Wuang et al. 2011). With focus on motor rehabilitation of youths with cerebral palsy, video games have been a motivating and enjoyable strategy used in therapies commonly termed virtual reality therapies (Deutsch et al. 2008; Golomb et al. 2010; Howcroft et al. 2012; Biddiss 2012). Likewise, these kinds of therapies for children with Down Syndrome have generated improvements on motor and sensory functions, providing varied array of activities and scenarios (Wuang et al. 2011). Researches point out virtual reality therapies are able to promote the neuroplasticity (cortical reorganization for the generation of synaptic potentiation), which can favour the motor learning, since video games stimulate important elements to develop this learning, such as motivation, reward, feedback, different levels of difficulty and repeated movement practice (Golomb et al. 2010; Biddiss 2012; Gatica-Rojas and Méndez-Rebolledo 2014).

Intelligent toys and robots present numerous features that become themselves potential and useful therapeutic tools, such as: availability; low cost; fun; functionality; anti-allergenic potential; possibility of adapting their control system, appearance, and exactness to the therapy needs; well acceptance by infants, children and adolescents; and finally, they don't get tired, bored or irritated (Komendziński et al. 2016). Toys and robots can also be used as manipulation tools allowing children with disabilities to participate in play or educational and therapeutic activities (Encarnação et al. 2014; Komendziński et al. 2016).

The field of the assistive robotics is a growing area of research and has become increasingly popular, taking into account the use of robots as therapeutic tools useful in several developmental disorders, as mediators of movement patterns, group activities, and social behaviours (François et al. 2009; Komendziński et al. 2016). Cognitive robots can be a promising therapeutic method for the treatment of developmental disorders and neurocognitive development, into semi-automated diagnostics and therapy and multimodal interactions in the promotion of attention, communication, and social skills, aiming the increase of rehabilitation outcomes (Komendziński et al. 2016). In addition, robot assistance is being incorporated in caregiving tasks in order to ease some of the burdens of providing care, thus opening up space and time for recreation and also improving the quality of life of those with impairments and their caregivers. However, robot caregivers are still restricted to small populations into experimental conditions, and as far as promising studies on positive interaction between children and robots raise, more robots can be designed and intended for assistance (Pearson and Borenstein 2013).

Among a variety of robotics applications, the robot-assisted repetitive motion training can be highlighted. These applications aim to encourage users to learn active control of movement. A use of this technology is in the hand motion training to improve functional handwriting in children with impaired motor skills, considering the relevance of a fluid and legible handwriting for people of all ages (Palsbo and Hood-Szivek 2012).

As aforementioned, play is of particular importance, especially in the early infancy, to the development of the motor and psychological healthy, in addition to the increase of quality of life, learning skills and social inclusion. Hence, children with impairments also should have the opportunity to experience an environment that supports the relevance of play and provides them with possibilities for doing so (Pearson and Borenstein 2013). In Autism Spectrum Disorder (ASD), different manifestation of the disorder can significantly affect the way in which children play with the toy (Andreae et al. 2014). Children with ASD usually understand play activities as learned routines, rather than an spontaneous expressions of themselves, due to the difficulty in communication and social interaction, which are common properties of this disorder (Giannopulu and Pradel 2010).

Robots with many sizes, shapes (anthropomorphic or not), ludic features and functions have been built to interact with children and adolescents diagnosed with Autism Spectrum Disorder to stimulate behavioural and social skills (Cabibihan et al. 2013). It is known that individuals with ASD express interest in robots (François et al. 2009) and interact positively with them, because they are simple, predictable and easier to understand than people (Duquette et al. 2008). Some researches bet on free game play in a child's spontaneous interaction with the robot, or "non-directive play" therapy (i.e. the child is the major leader for play), enabling a natural expression and engagement in social activities, which could lead to the development of social skills, in addition to encourage the child's proactivity and initiative-taking (François et al. 2009; Giannopulu and Pradel 2010). Thus, social robots are developed to provide a human-robot interaction more natural and instigating to stimulate in youths with ASD several abilities of the social behaviour which are reduced or absent due to this disorder, such as eye-gaze, touch, joint attention, engagement, imitation, verbal communication, among others (Kozima et al. 2009; Giannopulu and Pradel 2010; Robins et al. 2010; Kim et al. 2013; Andreae et al. 2014).

To illustrate, this chapter covers some examples of social assistive robots, recently developed in Brazilian universities (i.e. POB-BOT, Pomodoro and MARIA), for interaction with both physically impaired children and ASD children in order to develop their cognition and social skills. Features, such as their ludic aspect, their behaviours and the protocols used during the evaluations of the robot-volunteer interactions, are presented, together with the robots' functions.

2 The Robot Nino: Assisting Children with Severe Motor Impairment

Children develop their abilities in early age by exploration and discovery of the environment (Thomas 1993). However, some illnesses and impairments, such as cerebral palsy or muscular dystrophy, can prevent children to develop this exploration of the surroundings. This delay in exploration and discovery of the environment may compromise the social and cognitive development of these children, because it hinders self-discovery and leads to the constant need of someone to help them in several tasks.

That whole condition can make children feel a lack of independence, leading them to think that they always need external support to do things they need or want to. Even when they do not have prior mental illnesses, the physical disabilities can deprive them from having social experiences that would help them to develop socially or even cognitively. Ultimately, this makes the child believe in the idea that he or she cannot do things by themselves, a behaviour called "Learned Helplessness" (Albin et al. 1993).

According to Seligman (1992), a child with learned helplessness will avoid experiencing new things. This may hinder them to develop other skills, including cognitive and social skills. Other consequences are clinical depression and psychological problems related to the felling that they are unable to have a minimal control of their surrounding environment (Seligman 1992).

This scenario may lead the child to behave passively, being dependent and socially inactive. To confront this scenario, it is necessary to exploit other abilities those children have that can compensate their lacking capabilities, and thus enable them to interact with the environment (Scherzer 1990). By using alternative methods for environmental exploration, it is possible to develop their cognitive and social abilities and attenuate the learned helplessness, making them more independent and self-confident (Scherzer 1990; Albin et al. 1993).

One alternative method is to use any body movement, albeit limited, to tele-operate a robot that will serve as a proxy for world exploration. With this method, children can use the robot as an extension of their bodies, allowing them to indirectly modify the environment by themselves.

For that purpose, a hybrid accelerometer-sEMG (surface Electromyography) sensor is employed to capture body movements, and the Robot Nino is commanded to navigate through the environment. With this setup, a child can use his or her body to operate the Robot Nino and thus get involved in a play.

2.1 Robot Architecture

The robot Nino is based on the commercial mobile robot POB-BOT, which can also operate as a manipulator, since it has a robot arm with tweezers in its front. The robot has three servomotors: one to vertically move the tweezers; one for opening and closing the tweezers movement; and one used to adjust the camera orientation. The robot employs a differential drive system, which allows moving forward/backward and turning (POB Technology 2005).

To make the robot more appealing to children, its aesthetic was changed to create a "robotic clown" face, with springs and a pair of eyes. More details can be viewed in the overall functioning scheme, shown in Fig. 1.

To drive the robot Nino, it is necessary to acquire information about the child's movements or poses and translate them into commands for the robot. In order to acquire information about the child's movement during the experiments, a hybrid sensor containing both accelerometer and sEMG electrodes was used (Bortole 2011). The data acquired by the sensor is sent by Bluetooth connection to a host computer.

This sensor was chosen because it allows the capture of data from the body limbs the child can move. For example, if the child is able to flex or relax the hand muscles, the sEMG can be used to acquire information from this muscle. If otherwise the child is able to properly control the head's orientation, the accelerometer can be placed on the child's head to detect that movement. These inputs are ultimately translated into commands to the robot.

For simplicity an example using the accelerometer was considered in this application. As Fig. 1 illustrates, the sensor is attached on a cap, which is worn by the child.

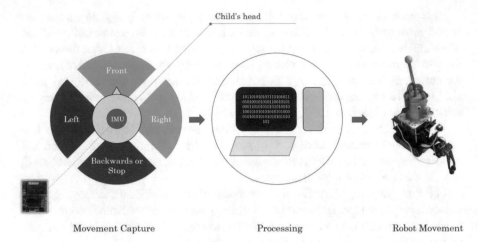

Child's head

Movement Capture   Processing   Robot Movement

Fig. 1 Nino overall system, in which a child uses head movements to control the mobile robot

To process the data acquired from the accelerometer and command the robot Nino, a computer with Bluetooth communication is adopted as the control unit, as shown by the diagram in Fig. 1.

As shown in the Fig. 1, the accelerometer detects the inclination of the child's head and sends to the computer. The computer process this data and translate into movement commands that are sent to the robot Nino. All sensor data is stored on the computer for future analysis.

The are four possible movements the child can perform: move the robot forward, backwards, to the right or to the left. In some experiments, the backwards movement is replaced by a stop command. In addition, if the child moves his or her head outside a safety zone, the robot stops.

The computer software is responsible for organizing the experiment and displaying the results after the whole test has completed. In addition, it also translates the head movement made by the child into robot movements. The software itself can be divided into four main parts, which are:

- Child registration: in this screen the therapist inform to the system the child's identification (following the Ethical Committee rules the real name of the child was not used, nor their initial name letters, instead the software just registered the child with a number). In addition, the therapist can also inform the type of experiment that is going to be done.
- Translation from the accelerometer board to the robot: the accelerometer sends signal to the computer, which, in turn, converts the information to the specific command to the robot and sends it to the robot.
- Log and report: since the computer makes the translation between the accelerometer board to the robot, the computer also register all the movements the child have made and makes a log that is available at the end of the experiment.

Fig. 2 Simple obstacle avoidance in first week test

Additionally, using the log information, all the relevant data about the experiment is organized in a HTML file that can be viewed by the therapist after the experiment.

2.2 Experiments

The volunteer group consisted of 9 children (7 with muscular dystrophy, 1 with cerebral palsy and 1 paraplegic). The experiments were conducted under the approval of the Ethical Committee of the Federal University of Espirito Santo, Brazil. All the volunteers were patients on the Centre of Physical Rehabilitation of Espirito Santo.

The experiments consisted of training how to manipulate the robot and, after that, perform some tasks of obstacle deviation, drawing on paper on the floor and controlling the robot movement to go through a path. Three different activities were carried out in three weeks of experiments with the volunteers. Each child was evaluated once or twice a week. Thus, the tasks were divided as follows:

- First Week: the task intended to make the child comfortable with the robot and to teach how to teleoperate it. The activity relied in moving the robot in a predetermined path that was easy to follow, with big obstacles that were not difficult to avoid. Figure 2 show a picture of this experiment.
- Second Week: the second activity was to draw anything on a big paper on the floor passing by some specific points marked on that paper. This activity required more attention and more control of the movements in order to achieve the goal than the first activity. This experiment is depicted in Fig. 3.

Fig. 3 Drawing on a paper on the floor in the second week

Fig. 4 Last week with a more complex obstacle avoidance task

- Third Week: the children had to accomplish an activity that consisted of guiding the robot through a path, but with more difficult obstacles. This time, such obstacles were smaller, and the path required the child to control the robot both forward and backwards. The obstacles were coloured blocks that guided the child through the correct path. Figure 4 show this last experiment.

2.3 Results

By analyzing the activities results, it was possible to infer if the children could use the robot better after having contact with it, or if they still experienced difficulties while manipulating it.

The results were based on how the children reacted to the robot and how long was the adaptation time. In addition, some specific goals were used to assess the children's achievement in the compliment of some tasks, such as drawing with the robot and moving the robot through obstacles.

Unfortunately, not all children could conclude the three activities. The results were analyzed by making the average value of the variables measured along the weeks.

To evaluate the system, one of the parameters analyzed was the valid movements, which are the ones that do not make the robot stop. This variable measures how confident the child is in using the system. When the child has to stop several times to understand better the robot movements, that means he or she has not comprehended the system to use it fluently. Therefore, a higher number of valid movements in comparison with non-valid movements means the child could understand better the system.

Another variable used as statistics was the time needed to complete the task and the number of valid movements per second. The tests were designed in a way that the number of movements per second is inversely proportional to the level of confidence of the child and directly proportional to the goal complexity.

Finally, to evaluate how well the children performed, the Goal Attainment Scale, known as GAS, was used. GAS is a scale that can convert qualitative analysis into quantitative analysis by focusing on the tasks of the evaluated goals (McDougall 2007; Krasny-Pacini et al. 2013).

Four variables were used to compare the evolution of the children while using the robot during the three-week experiment. The first of them is the time needed to accomplish the goals; the second is the number of movements per second; the third is the ratio between valid movements and the total movements and, finally, the GAS score.

The information provided by the *time to complete the tasks* tells how the child is getting used to the system and how many seconds the child needs to complete the task, as the tasks complexity impacts in the time needed to perform the whole experiment. Therefore, since the experiments were each week more difficult, the time needed is expected to be bigger throughout the weeks. The evolution of each child is shown in Table 1.

When the children are more comfortable and understand the robot movements, they tend to make less *movements per second*. This can indicate if the child is understanding how to control the robot. As Table 2 shows, from the first to the second week, there was an increase in the number of moves per second, and, in the third week, there was a decrease compared with the two previous weeks (in average). The task of the second week (drawing passing by specific points) needed more movements when compared with the task of the first week (training how to use the robot avoiding simple obstacles). This explains why the children had to make more movements per second.

Furthermore, comparing the first week with the third week, that had similar tasks, but with different complexities (in the third week the child had to pass through small obstacles, which was more difficult), it was possible to verify that some children could achieve the goals making less moves per second.

Table 1 Time needed to accomplish the tasks in seconds

Number	1st week	2nd week	3rd week
1	89	320	N/A
2	N/A	139	N/A
3	N/A	N/A	376
4	87	N/A	N/A
5	265	92	N/A
6	142	183	264
7	243	304	801
8	N/A	324	N/A
9	349	144	N/A
Average	196	215	480

Table 2 Movements per second

Number	1st week	2nd week	3rd week
1	0.80	1.86	N/A
2	N/A	2.28	N/A
3	N/A	N/A	1.44
4	1.47	N/A	N/A
5	1.41	2.32	N/A
6	2.30	1.40	0.89
7	2.98	1.64	1.97
8	N/A	1.49	N/A
9	0.63	1.56	N/A
Average	1.60	1.79	1.43

Table 3 Ratio between valid movements and total movements

Number	1st week	2nd week	3rd week
1	56.53%	74.78%	N/A
2	N/A	79.30%	N/A
3	N/A	N/A	78.37%
4	70.69%	N/A	N/A
5	89.81%	76.35%	N/A
6	80.43%	89.58%	85.41%
7	75.43%	73.85%	68.33%
8	N/A	82.49%	N/A
9	85.80%	87.01%	N/A
Average	76.45%	80.48%	77.93%

The value of *movements per second* provides a more accurate idea of how the child is understanding the robot. Basically, if the child needs to make more movements, either the task is more difficult or he or she is having more difficulty in operating the system, as detailed in Table 3.

If the child is learning how to use the robot, throughout the time the tendency is that the child increases the percentage of valid movements when compared with the first contact with the robot. As Table 3 shows, in the second and third weeks the ratio was higher.

Table 4 GAS values for each child in each task

Number	1st week	2nd week	3rd week
1	56.53%	74.78%	N/A
2	N/A	79.30%	N/A
3	N/A	N/A	78.37%
4	70.69%	N/A	N/A
5	89.81%	76.35%	N/A
6	80.43%	89.58%	85.41%
7	75.43%	73.85%	68.33%
8	N/A	82.49%	N/A
9	85.80%	87.01%	N/A
Average	76.45%	80.48%	77.93%

Comparing the third and second weeks, there is a reduction in the average percentage of valid movements. However, this is mainly due to the nature of the task, since the last week had a task that required to stop the robot more times compared to the second week. However, this reduction is relatively small, since the second week required much less stop commands to the robot. For the volunteer #7, the value was smaller compared with the first week and for the volunteer #6, it was smaller compared with both previous weeks, being the best case.

Finally, another analysis that can be made is using the GAS score for each child in the three weeks, which are shown in Table 4. The GAS variation shows the overall improvement of the child over the weeks to accomplish the tasks. The GAS value had the tendency of rising (comparing the first and last week), which has similar kind of test (obstacle avoidance), but the last being much more difficult it is possible to see that the GAS had improved. This is an indicator that the child could manipulate the robot better in the last week, even with a harder task.

The comparison between the second and third week is not very adequate, since the nature of the tasks are quite different, being the drawing activity much simpler than the obstacle avoidance, which is much more complex.

2.4 Discussion

The experiments show that, at the end of the third week, the children got more adapted to the robot. In addition, not only the children, but also parents, caregivers and physiotherapists reported the children got happy using the robot and this helped them to become even more engaged in their physiotherapy sessions.

Some movements they were required to do to complete the tasks were similar to the movements they needed to do in their regular physiotherapy. Although this was not intentionally designed, it demonstrated that the children were more engaged in doing these movements (that could be previously very difficult for them) just because they were interacting with the robot. Then, the robot was giving them an entertaining time, adding to the fact they could feel better, since they could do tasks they would not be able without the external support of the robot.

When impaired children can interact better with their surroundings, they can improve their socialization, increase their self-esteem and have more independence for some tasks. All this context increases the quality of life of those physically impaired children, including those who have some psychological and emotional impairments due to the physical one.

Therefore, by using robotics, those children can manipulate more their surroundings and this can have a positive impact in their development, even in areas such as learning and social interaction, that are also important for the human development.

Another important fact is the ludic aspect of the robot, that helped the children to deal with their physiotherapy tasks, since the robot, in some way, made them make movements they should do in their therapies, even some movements they found very hard to do.

This robot was greatly accepted and the experiments show that, since the robot was seen as a friendly toy, with no child presenting fear. This is an important aspect considering the ludic robot, whose main goal is to help those children to achieve more independence by interacting wirelessly with a robot and indirectly with their surroundings.

3   Pomodoro, An Affordable Social Robot

The positive experience with Nino led the development of the Pomodoro robot (Fig. 5), which serves as an affordable robot base for assistive applications. The robot's body uses flat acrylic parts that can be easily replicated, and the circuit board is based on a single microcontroller to reduce costs. Pomodoro is designed with round shapes to not harm the user, and uses vivid colours to draw children's attention.

Pomodoro's hardware architecture consists of two parts: one integrated hardware running a supervisor software, and one smartphone implementing the control architecture. The supervisor's purpose is to read the sensors and activate the actuators. Furthermore, the supervisor can operate in two modes: non-autonomous (blindly executing the smartphone's commands), and semi-autonomous (it still requires the smartphone's commands to operate, but triggers simple reactive behaviours to avoid falling and obstacles).

The adoption of a smartphone as the embedded computer has improved Pomodoro's functionality, connectivity and energy efficiency, while reducing the costs. The smartphone was chosen over other embedded solutions, such as the Raspberry PI, because it employs a set of devices and interfaces that can be exploited by robotics, such as the processing unit, touchscreen, camera, accelerometer, gyroscope, audio input and output, and wireless communications. Additionally, the Android mobile operating system provides speech recognition and synthesis, which are useful for creating natural Human-Robot Interaction (HRI). Android is also

Fig. 5 Pomodoro robot
showing a "surprised"
expression (pictogram)

supported by a large developer community, which provides free and commercial software tools and libraries that ease the creation of new applications.

On Pomodoro, the smartphone is positioned over an articulated base, as shown on Fig. 5, which allows the robot to change the smartphone's orientation (*pan* and *tilt*) and its camera field-of-view, which might be required by some tasks.

Another important feature of Pomodoro is the Control Architecture (Alves and Ferasoli Filho 2016), which was developed to allow the robot to interact with people in a natural fashion. The next session describes the design of Pomodoro's Control Architecture.

3.1 Control Architecture

The control architecture was created to enable a rich and meaningful interaction with children while executing a task. Hence, the architecture must provide algorithms that address the main task and that support HRI. To this end, Pomodoro adopts a hybrid, bio-inspired control architecture composed of both deliberative and reactive layers that mimic elements found in animals.

Another distinguishing feature of this control architecture is its distributed nature. Each module is implemented as an independent software application, which allows the architecture to exploit the parallel computing capabilities of the host machine, reduces the scope of software failures (i.e. failure in one module, such as crashing, does not halt other modules), and provides a flexible structure where modules can be added or removed without the need of recompiling the whole system.

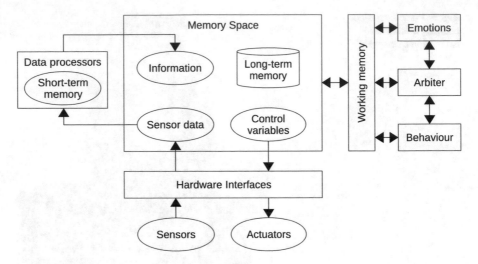

Fig. 6 Intelligent control architecture

As Fig. 6 illustrates, the control architecture is composed of four main modules, namely memory space, hardware interfaces, data processors, and controller.

The *memory space* is inspired on the psychological concept of modal memory (Atkinson and Shiffrin 1968). It serves for two purposes: as a *communication mean* and to *store data*. As such, it divides the memory in three types:

Sensory memory: captures sensory *stimuli*, which are erased if not accessed by any process.
Short-term memory: also known as *working memory*, it stores the relevant *stimulus* and data about the current task.
Long-term memory: stores a set of organized data for a undetermined time.

The *hardware interfaces* may either read and decode sensory data or drive the actuators. Hardware interfaces thus "produce" decoded sensor data at the memory space with a short duration, usually 1 s, and "consume" information about the setpoints of its actuators.

Data processors are the modules that reads and process sensory data to produce useful information. Hence, these modules provide data-processing services to the controller, thus reducing the controller complexity.

The controller is the main part of the architecture, which actually controls the mobile robot. It is composed of three layers, as shown by Fig. 6, namely *behaviours*, *arbiter* and *emotion*.

The *behaviours* uses a combination of Finite State Machines (FSM) (Arkin 1998) to represent higher level actions and their transition, and motor schema model (Arkin 1989) to represent lower level actions and their relation to external stimuli.

On common conditions, only one behaviour is active at a given time. However, there might be situations where two or more behaviours may compete to control the robot. In such cases, the *Arbiter* is responsible for deciding which behaviour should have precedence in controlling the mobile robot, which are categorized within three priority layers:

Security: is the highest priority layer and encompasses the behaviours that guarantees the robot integrity, such as fall and obstacle avoidance.

Regulation: is inspired by the homeostasis observed in living beings, which is the ability of a biological system to maintain stable and relatively constant their internal conditions by means of regulating mechanisms (Guyton and Hall 2006). For a robotic system, regulation is a set of behaviours that maintains the operability of the robot, such as keeping the battery charge at secure levels.

Task: is concerned with the global objective of the robot and thus contains the behaviours needed to achieve it.

The *artificial emotions* were added to the controller in order to make the interaction with children more engaging and natural (Breazeal and Brooks 2004). For this application, eleven emotions were considered. From these emotions, *happy*, *sad*, *disgust*, *fear*, *anger* and *surprise* are analogous to the six "universal emotions" of Paul Ekman (1999). The emotions *excited* and *calm* are considered respectively as "high-aroused" and "low-aroused" happiness, while *depressed* is a "acute" sadness. The *sleepy* emotion indicates fatigue. When no emotion is detected, the *neutral* emotion is selected.

The artificial emotions are displayed by the robot through body movements, sounds, and pictograms displayed on the smartphone screen. Each artificial emotion has a corresponding pictogram, which eases the interpretation of the robot's emotional state.

3.2   Pomodoro As a Toy for Aiding Children with ASD

As mentioned in Sect. 1, robots have been successfully used as aid in the therapy of children with ASD. Thus, to demonstrate Pomodoro's features as an assistive robot, as well as the control architecture, an application of social interaction was proposed. The robot acts as an "artificial pet" to play with the child using pre-built ludic activities.

Some modules were implemented for the control architecture presented in Sect. 3.1 to enable the robot to perform the required tasks. Thus, two hardware interfaces were developed:

Robot body: used to send commands to Pomodoro's embedded supervisor to read sensors and drive actuators.

Robot head: used to acquire images and touch information from the smartphone, as well to indicate which robot faces (pictograms) to show.

In order to process data from the smartphone camera, provided by the *Robot head* hardware interface, the following data processor was created:

Image processing: used for detecting faces (with OpenCV library[1]) and Aug-
    mented Reality Markers (using NyARToolkit library[2]). Face detection is used
    to enable the robot to detect the presence of a user and to adjust its "face"
    (smartphone) orientation to gaze at the user. Marker detection is used to
    implement the card-matching game, which will be addressed bellow.

The implemented behaviours are related to a given layer of the arbiter, discussed
on Sect. 3.1. For the *task layer*, the four following behaviours were created:

Search person: the robot moves itself and searches for a child through face
    detection.
Touch play: the robot asks the child to touch its face, i.e. the smartphone screen.
    The goal of this play is to lessen the aversion children with ASD feel about
    touching others.
Dance play: the robot starts playing music and moving, and invites the child to
    dance with it. The goal of this play is to help children to learn to pay attention to
    simple verbal commands, and to use his or her body as means of expression.
Card play: The robot asks the child to play a card-matching game to teach some
    basic concepts with picture cards. In this game, the robot asks the child to show a
    previous known card by vocalizing the name of the card and showing its picture
    on the smartphone screen. If the child shows the right card, the robot will praise;
    if a wrong card is shown, the robot will console and encourage the child to redo
    the choice.

Due to the simplicity of the robot and the application, the regulatory layer
contains a single behaviour: *Sleep*, which is activated when the robot emotion is
classified as "tired", "sad" or "depressed", and its magnitude e_m is larger than 0.75.
When active, this behaviour "recovers" the robots humour to "happy".

In this application, the security layer is used to avoid falling and thus have the
avoid danger behaviour. This behaviour detects when the robot is getting on the
edge of the workspace by using its infrared ground sensors, and activates the motors
to ensure the robot will not advance the edges and fall.

3.3   Pilot Study

To validate the assistive application, the robot Pomodoro was experimented with
children, which are the target public. The goal of the pilot study was to verify if
the robot would function properly in an uncontrolled environment, and to gather the
opinion of the therapists. Thus, the experiments were performed with two partner
institutions from the state of Sao Paulo, Brazil: RASC and AFAPAB.

---

[1] OpenCV Library: http://opencv.org/
[2] NyARToolkit lybrary: http://nyatla.jp/nyartoolkit/wp/

Fig. 7 An experiment session where a child with ASD was playing the card-matching game with the robot Pomodoro

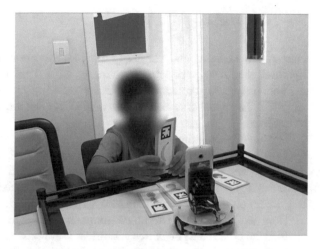

RASC (Christian Socio-educational Assistance Network) is a private, non-profit institution which provides shelter to 4–10 years old boys. This institution allowed five typically developed children aged from 2 to 8 years old to participate on the experiments.

AFAPAB (Association of Family and Friends of People with Autism of Bauru) is a non-profit association which provides services for children diagnosed with ASD in order to help them to develop language, behaviour and socialization to improve their quality of life.

After meeting with the administrative and pedagogic teams of the institution, in which the robot was presented and explained, the institution selected four children with ASD whose developmental level was compatible with the games performed by the robot. All children were calm, non-aggressive, and had good social development. Even though the institution works with both male and female, unintentionally the four kids were male. Figure 7 shows one child playing the card-matching game with the robot.

Unlike the experiments performed at RASC, in which the smartphone's default female voice was used for speech synthesis, the experiment carried out at AFAPAB had the smartphone using a male voice. This was requested by the technicians of AFAPAB, who reported that children exhibited apathy for the female voice.

All the experimental sessions were performed by the technicians from both RASC and AFAPAB, who did not have formal training in assistive robotics. The technicians were provided a brief 5 min explanation on the operation, which were enough for them to feel familiar with the robot, even though that was the first time they saw a robot.

The parents or legal guardians of all volunteers signed an informed consent and the experiments were previously approved by the Ethical Committee of the Federal University of Espirito Santo, Brazil, partner of this research.

3.4 Discussion

During the experiments, the robot Pomodoro operated properly, even though lightning conditions varied and were sub-optimal. This was achieved by employing markers as means for recognizing and classifying the picture cards during card activities. The robot was also able to navigate in the workspace and to detect falls as expected.

The use of pictograms instead of real faces was well received by technicians, as well as the synthetic voices, both male and female, which were considered "firm and safe". The lack of emotive expression in the synthesized voices was not considered a problem for the technicians, which reported that a "constant" speech was easier to be understood by children with underdeveloped social skills.

Thus, the simplicity of the pictograms and the clarity of the speech synthesis enabled the creation of objective and direct ludic activities, which allowed the creation of a "communication channel" with the children. However, the effectiveness of such channel depends on the fast robot response to the stimuli provided by children. For example, the need to quickly recognize the card being shown and promptly reacting to it. If the robot takes too long to respond, the child will understand that a failure has occurred in the communication channel and will also disperse his or her attention.

The technicians from AFAPAB observed that the ease of use of the robot would allow children to participate in therapy with the help of a caregiver with no formal instruction on the area. At first, the robot would be used by the therapists to teach the child. When the child feels habituated to the robot, the procedures could be performed at home with the help of the parents or a caregiver. This way, the technicians could work on the development of new skills, while parents and caregivers could help maintain the already learned skills.

Other positive point observed by therapists is the fact that the robot does not "get tired" of its repetitive tasks. In general, psycho-pedagogical activities with children with ASD are repetitive and tiresome for the therapists, who are also subject to emotional fatigue when the child is not behaving properly. The robot, on the other hand, does not demonstrated tiredness and repeat the tasks in a constant fashion, without changing the voice tone or slowing movements. This constancy eases the therapists to carry out longer activities with the child.

The technicians from both institutes noted that the robot only moved while searching for the child to start playing. Once the child was within the robot's field of view, it stops moving. This lack of movement is not desirable, since it does not appeal to children. Therefore, future development of the robot Pomodoro will add body movements to the robot during activities.

The application received overall positive feedback from the technicians from both institutes. The robot operated properly without performing any undesired behaviour, and was able to quickly respond to the children' stimuli. As a work-in-progress, this research will further improve the robot activities, such as adding more movement to the robot, as well as expanding the number of picture cards for the card-matching game.

4   MARIA: A Social Robot Aiding Children with ASD

Another robot that is used in the therapy of children with ASD is MARIA (acronym for *Mobile Autonomous Robot for Interaction with Autistics*). MARIA is 1.35 m tall and very colourful, a feature that attracts the attention of children, both those typically developed and those diagnosed with ASD.

Unlike robots Nino and Pomodoro, which are small robots designed to be used in small areas, MARIA was conceived to be able to operate with the same conditions as the children. Thus, MARIA is able to move bigger objects, and has enough space in its structure to embed additional sensors, providing new possibilities of interaction and ludic plays that are only possible with a children-sized robot.

MARIA core structure is a Pioneer 3-DX robot that, just like Nino and Pomodoro, uses a differential drive system to move. This robot is equipped with eight front sonars and a laser rangefinder. When building MARIA's body, a multimedia system was added to allow it to reproduce videos and sounds.

The toy-like aspect was created by using colourful papers covering cardboards, springs and metallic paper with extruded polystyrene balls representing its hands covered in aluminum foil. Eyelash, eyelids, a wig, mouth, eyes, nose and a brilliant metallic paper of aluminum foil face was all designed in order to make the robot as most colourful as possible.

Figure 8 shows how MARIA looks like a robotic toy, specially due to its square-shaped geometry.

Most of the sensors attached to MARIA's structure were employed to allow the robot to detect where the child was located and to entertain the child during the robot-child interaction.

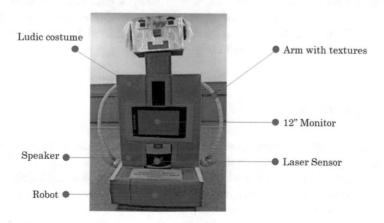

Fig. 8 MARIA robot

The main sensor of MARIA is a 180-degree SICK®laser rangefinder that is used to identify the child position inside a controlled environment. Inside this area and under the robot vision range, only the child can be located. So, the robot uses the controllers to reach him/her always keeping a safe distance.

Regarding the other devices that work as entertaining devices for children while interacting with the robot, the multimedia system consists of speakers and a display that exhibit colourful movies and cartoons. All this multimedia part was build to entertain the child and allow them to feel more comfortable with the robot.

4.1 Software

MARIA runs different software that helped to deliver the robotic toy experience to the child. Although there is an autonomous control mode, the tests presented here were conducted using only manual control.

The robot has an internal computer that provides VNC (Virtual Networking Computing) remote access. By using the VNC, it is possible to control the animations the robot displays on the screen. In addition, the robot movements are generated by the inner computer of the robot, which can be also remotely controlled by the means of the VNC. The master computer, which is commanded by the therapist/researcher, provides the commands to the robot. At the same time, another therapist/researcher can play with the child and with the robot to try the social engagement (researcher-robot-child).

The therapist/researcher uses the keyboard of the master computer to control the robot, which has an internal computer connected to the motor drive circuitry. The directional arrows of the keyboard are used to control the robot directions. Thus, while pressing them the robot moves reaching the maximum defined speed after some seconds holding the button. Once the button is released the robot slows down until next command or until it stops completely.

4.2 Experiments

Two group of children participated in the experiments, one with five typically developing children (TD) and another with five children with ASD. All volunteers (when applicable) and their parents or legal guardians signed an informed consent and the experiments were previously approved by the Ethical Committee of the Federal University of Espirito Santo.

During the experiments, the robot has a special area inside the room, from which it cannot leave (Fig. 9). Due to safety concerns, no automatic control was used in these experiments. Instead, the robot was remotely controlled by the therapist or caretaker according to the child behaviour. In addition, parents and/or caretakers always were present during the tests.

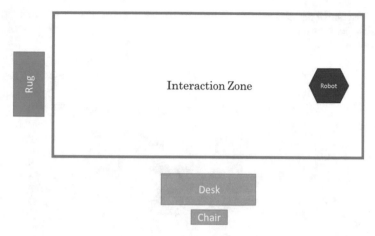

Fig. 9 Setup of the room where the tests took place

The experiments consisted of two phases: (1) self-presentation, in which the robot first makes a self-presentation; (2) direct interaction, in which the robot makes a free interaction with the child. The first part of the test was created in order to make the child feel more comfortable and to introduce the robot to them.

At the beginning of the test, the child is asked to stay outside a rectangle marked region of the room. Since the robot cannot go outside this area, if the child feels fear, he or she can run out of the marked area, so the robot will stop at the internal border. The robot was covered with a sheet and was placed at one extremity of the test area. Parents and caretakers were asked to sit comfortably with the child in a rug that is located outside the marked area, in the opposite extremity to the robot. They waited for the robot to be uncovered.

After the robot is uncovered by one of the therapists/researchers, it starts moving towards the place where the rug is. Simultaneously it displays an animation with video and sound content. This animation was selected by asking the parents previously which kind of cartoon and animations their children like. While the robot exhibits the animation, it also moves towards the child, but not in a single movement. First it moves 90 cm until a marked dot, inside the limit region. In that place, it spins 360°, so the child can see the whole robot with all colours and shapes. The robot, then moves straight more 90 cm, stops and spins 360°, but now counter clockwise. Finally the robot makes its last movement of the first phase, which is move more 90 cm and stop at 30 cm away from the child. This first phase is represented by Fig. 10.

The second part is already an interaction phase. In this phase, the robot has already been presented to the child, which means it is not a completely unknown object. Always the researcher is controlling the robot, but also observing the child. Therefore, the therapist can determine the movements the robot should make to allow the child interact better with the robot. To complement the interaction aid, another researcher (and sometimes the parents) also stays with the child, encouraging him/her and playing with the child and the robot.

Fig. 10 Diagram of the self
presentation performed by
robot MARIA

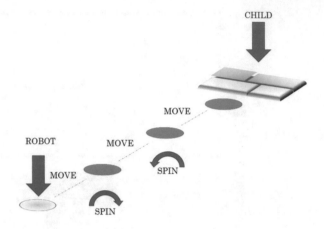

4.3   Evaluation Scales and Tools

During the tests, in the first phase (self-presentation), the children's behaviour is observed, in order to, analyze if they were looking and paying attention to the robot. On the other phase (direct interaction), it was analyzed how the children behaved regarding on touching the robot and imitating and answering the commands of the mediator (researcher).

To evaluate the children reaction to the robot and their performance while interacting with it, two metric scales were used. Besides those scales, informal conversation with parents was also taken to know what they felt about the robot. The first scale used is the aforementioned GAS, which was also used by robot Nino.

Hence, once the accomplishment performance is made qualitatively by the therapist or caretaker, the scale allows the conversion between such information into numbers. The evaluation guidelines are given using Table 5.

The other scale used to evaluate the application is the System Usability Scale (SUS). SUS is a way to measure the system usability with a device or software by answering standardized scored question. The question answers vary from "strongly disagree" (with value equals 1) until "strongly agree" (with value equals 5). Therefore, the answer can vary between these two values (1 to 5) representing how the user agrees with the information shown in the sentence.

An interesting feature of this scale is that the even questions are written in a inverse way from the odd questions. This helps to understand if the user could really understand and answer the questionnaire, since it is expected that the complementary questions (with the same idea, but written in opposite way) should have different answers.

The standardized ten question are (Lewis and Sauro 2009):

1. I think that I would like to use this robot frequently.
2. I found the robot unnecessarily complex.

Table 5 GAS table used to quantify the goals

Quality	Score	Look	Touch	Imitate
Worst	−2	Look to the robot at least 30 s and fell fear	Stay away from the robot and do not touch it	Keep sit down, even if the mediator encourages to interact
Worse	−1	Look to the robot at least 30 s and show no reaction	Touch the robot for less than 5 s	Stand up, but do not show any interest in move, even encouraged by the mediator
Expected	0	Look to the robot for more than 30 s and keep looking to the monitor without interest	Touch the robot for more than 5 s	Make the same interaction movement showed by the mediator for at least 20 s
Better	+1	Look to the robot for more than 30 s and pay attention to the monitor	Touch the robot for more than 5 s and pay attention to the monitor	Make the same interaction movement showed by the mediator for more than 20 s
Best	+2	Look to the robot for more than 30 s and move him/herself towards the robot	Touch the robot for more than 5 s and try to play with it	Make the same interaction movement showed by the mediator and imitate the robot next him/her

3. I thought the robot was easy to use.
4. I think that I would need the support of a technical person to be able to use this robot.
5. I found the various functions in this robot were well integrated.
6. I thought there was too much inconsistency in this robot.
7. I would imagine that most people would learn to use this robot very quickly.
8. I found the robot very cumbersome to use.
9. I felt very confident using the robot.
10. I needed to learn a lot of things before I could get going with this robot.

As the list shows, the odd questions are written in a "positive" way, while the even questions are written in a "negative" way, although they are asking essentially the same thing.

After scoring each question, it is necessary to calculate the overall score of the questionnaire. This is done by employing the equations given by Lewis and Sauro (2009), which returns values from 0 to 100. However, this value is neither a percentile rank nor they form a linear relation, the relation between the SUS score and the percentile rank is not linear, with the average equals 68 (Brooke 2013).

4.4 Results

The results were positive for most children who took part of the tests. From the 10 children who participated, half of them were diagnosed with ASD, while the other half were typically developed. In Tables 6 and 7 the values of the GAS score are shown, respectively for ASD children and TD group.

The GAS average score for ASD children was 60.94 ± 18.41, while for TD children it was 70.98 ± 6.92. Therefore, both groups were above the average (50%) in this scale. This indicate a positive result, since both groups could achieve above the average score.

Regarding the SUS scores, they are indicated in Tables 8 and 9, respectively for ASD and TD children. This SUS questionnaire was answered by the parents, since it evaluates how the robot is useful and easy to be used by the parent/therapists to help their children, and due to the fact most children may not understand the questions.

The SUS average values (62 for ASD children and 63,5 for TD children) indicates that, for both groups, the robot can be improved in its functionality and usability, since although the values were close to the average (68), they did not reach the average.

Table 6 Results of the GAS for ASD children

Goals	ASD1	ASD2	ASD3	ASD4	ASD5
Look	+1	+1	+2	+1	−1
Touch	−2	+2	+2	+2	0
Imitate	−1	+2	+2	+2	−1
GAS	40.88	72.8	77.36	72.8	40.88

Table 7 Results of the GAS for TD children

Goals	TD1	TD2	TD3	TD4	TD5
Look	+1	+2	+1	+1	+1
Touch	+2	+2	+2	+2	−1
Imitate	+2	+2	+2	+2	+2
GAS	72.8	77.36	72.8	72.8	59.12

Table 8 SUS results for the ASD children

Question	ASD1	ASD2	ASD3	ASD4	ASD5
#1	3	5	3	3	3
#2	3	1	3	2	2
#3	2	5	2	5	5
#4	5	1	4	1	1
#5	4	5	4	3	3
#6	3	1	3	3	3
#7	2	5	2	4	4
#8	5	1	4	2	2
#9	3	5	3	3	3
#10	5	1	5	2	2
SUS	32.5	100.0	37.5	70.0	70.0

Table 9 SUS results for the TD children

Question	TD1	TD2	TD3	TD4	TD5
#1	3	5	5	5	2
#2	3	1	2	1	2
#3	2	5	5	5	4
#4	5	3	4	4	5
#5	4	5	4	5	5
#6	3	1	3	1	2
#7	2	2	4	2	4
#8	5	1	2	2	2
#9	3	5	4	5	2
#10	5	1	3	4	5
SUS	32.5	87.5	70.0	75.0	52.5

4.5 Discussion

Most children had a good results with the robot MARIA, mainly according with the GAS and through talking with the parents after the experiments. Only one child rejected the interaction with the robot, while the others either enjoyed and interacted directly or, after some encouragement, relaxed and eventually had an interaction with the robot.

The behaviour among the typically developed children were positive and they enjoyed playing with the robot. In the other group, some children need encouragement and all children but one interacted with the robot. This showed that the robot could attract the child's attention and make them have a positive reaction towards the robot.

The robot MARIA was widely accepted by children of both group. Nine out of ten children accepted it, showing little to no fear and reacting the robot either spontaneously or after encouragement. Only one child, from the ASD group, did not interacted with the robot even after encouragement.

The GAS results were over the mean average for both groups. However, the SUS results were below the average value, which indicate that the children from both groups could accomplish the goals in a better than expected way, but the robot still needs some improvements, in order to the parents find it easy to be used by them to help their children.

Two different kinds of interaction could be done using MARIA. One is the self-presentation, when the robot introduces itself. Although the children acts as a spectator in this test, his/her first contact with the robot is important to prepare them for the next interaction phase.

In the second interaction phase, the robot and the child interact directly and it is possible also to involve another person, usually a researcher, a parent or a caregiver, to interact together. Thus, it is possible to analyze a child-robot interaction and a triad interaction (child-robot plus another person). Some interesting features of MARIA that help in this context can be highlighted, which are:

- Height: the robot has the approximate height of a 7–8 year old child (1.35 m). This helped children to interact in the same level with the robot. Authors such as Giullian et al. (2010) suggest that if the robot is too small the child can be interested in analyze the robot as an object to be examined regarding its mechanical parts instead of interacting with it. On the other hand, if the robot is bigger than the child it could make them fell afraid and they could avoid interaction due to this fear.
- Mixed anthropomorphic and non-anthropomorphic features: due to the fact the robot mixes both features, it becomes at the same time a social robot, due to the anthropomorphic features, but with less complexity, due to its non-anthropomorphic features, making it easier for the child to understand and making them more curious, since the non-anthropomorphic features explore the mechanical aspect of the robot (Paron-Wildes 2005).
- Multimedia content and self-presentation: both elements were important for the child to get used with the robot and to have a first contact before interacting directly with it. This feature helped to understand if the child was with fear or if he/she was felling relaxed. This also was used as a guideline for the researcher that was tele-operating the robot and for the next phase, which has a direct interaction between the child and the robot.

Considering the whole aspect of the research, it is possible to conclude the children had benefit using the robot, even in this pilot study. A more complete robot, with more sensors and behaviours will be developed as an evolution of this first version. The new robot will consider aspects that can be improved, such as inserting into the robot sensors that perceive the touching among other children's behaviour or interaction intentions and reactions, and automatizing the control, making the robot fully autonomous.

5   Final Considerations

Robotics can be a very useful tool for helping children with impairments to improve their cognitive and social skills. As shown in this chapter, different approaches for distinct kinds of impairment have to be addresses in order to help those children. To physically impaired children, the robot would work as a way of making them more independent by minimizing the effects of their impairment in some of their daily tasks. That is the way how Nino was used, in which children can draw, even if they were not able to use their hands to guide a pencil. For this end, Nino aided by allowing them to draw and play with the robot using the abilities they still have – in that case, the head movement. Thus, they can do interactions with the environment that they were not able and that makes them fell more comfortable and less dependent and limited.

Another application of robotics to help children with disabilities can be viewed in the use of the robot Pomodoro, that works as an assistive robot for children with

ASD with different behaviours, such as *searching person, touch play, dance play, card play* and *sleep*. In this case, the robot acts as an "artificial pet" and helps ASD children by playing with them ludic activities. To this end, there is a intelligent control architecture that considers different layers for processing the information and creating the necessary behaviour to the robot.

The robot MARIA also works with children with ASD. In this case, the approach used was to interact with the child by using self-presentation and playing with the child together with a mediator inside a controlled room. A second researcher controlled the robot manually respecting the limit the robot should stay inside the room. In this kind of approach, it is possible to evaluate the children interaction after a self-presentation and during a direct interaction with the robot, which was also made together with a mediator (researcher).

As shown, robots for rehabilitation (regarding socially and cognitive aspects) have to be adapted to the kind of children they will work with. In addition, the tasks the children will perform with the robot also have big influence on the robot building, programming, setting of behaviours, among other features. Therefore, building a social robot should consider a series of features that ranges from the physical structure to the behaviour and safety.

The robot should also be flexible regarding the different features of the group it will work with. For example, the robot should be able to have different behaviours and several elements that children fell attractive. Some children may not find some of the elements attractive, but will find others as attractive, and vice-versa. In addition, the multimedia elements are great features that allow different stimuli to the child, and with this flexibility, it is possible to work with a larger group and customize the protocol for each child, if necessary, making the experiment more adequate to each child and increasing the chances of success in interaction.

In the literature, there are several robots that are used to help children develop cognitively and socially, approaching different kinds of impairments. In the work of Cook et al. (2002), a robotic arm is used to help children with physical impairments, which may improve social and cognitive aspects and the learned helplessness. Other works, such as Kim et al. (2013), Kozima et al. (2009), Cabibihan et al. (2013), Michaud and Clavet (2001), and Valadão et al. (2016) show the use of robots for ASD children to develop their social abilities, by teaching and stimulating their social and cognitive skills, using different approaches and kind of robots.

Thus, the use of robots opens great possibilities to help interaction with impaired children, since they can be viewed as toy and they are in most cases friendly and less complex as humans in terms of expression. Creativity and protocol customization help the robot to achieve success in interacting with the robot. Although challenging due to different public and aspects that is needed to deal with, it is also very rewarding, since the robots can give an aid in the development of those children.

To conclude, it is important to mention that the therapists' support is always necessary, since the robot is a tool used to open new possibilities as a tool for interacting with children. The robot may help the process, but the therapy conduction should be given by the therapist. In this sense, the robot is a friendly tool that can help to optimize this process, not to automate it. In fact, the health professional or therapist are attentive and careful with the individual needs of each infant-juvenile patient, knowing how to select the most adequate tool, or to adapt it according to the needs, goals, age, motor abilities and emotional and cognitive development, besides supervising its usage and feedback (You et al. 2005; Biddiss 2012; Sposito et al. 2016). Therefore, it is prudent to emphasize the important participation of the health professionals or therapists in play-assisted therapies, because they ought to be sensitive to observe, listen to and answer the infant-juvenile patients, reflecting their feelings or emotional behaviours, in order to aid them to have a better understanding of themselves and the experiences they are going through (François et al. 2009).

Acknowledgements Authors would like to thank all the volunteer children and theirs parents for participating in the tests, the Associations and their therapists, for helping in conducting the tests, the Brazilian agencies that promote research (CNPq/CAPES, FAPES and FAPESP), for the technical, scientific and financial support.

References

Albin RW, Bateman V, Dunst CJ, Gordon NJ, Gibbs B, Lerner E, Irvine B (1993) Families, disability, and empowerment: active coping skills and strategies for family interventions. Paul H Brookes Pub Co, Baltimore

Alves, SFdR, Ferasoli Filho H (2016) Intelligent control architecture for assistive mobile robots. J Control Autom Electr Syst 27(5):515–526

Andreae HE, Andreae PM, Low J, Brown D (2014) A study of auti: a socially assistive robotic toy. In: Proceedings of the 2014 conference on interaction design and children (IDC'14). ACM, New York, pp 245–248

Arkin RC (1989) Motor schema – based mobile robot navigation. Int J Rob Res 8(4):92–112

Arkin RC (1998) Behavior-based robotics. MIT Press, Cambridge

Atkinson RC, Shiffrin RM (1968) Human memory: a proposed system and its control processes. Psychol Learn Motiv 2:89–195

Biddiss E (2012) Should we integrate video games into home-based rehabilitation therapies for cerebral palsy? Future Neurol 7(5):515–518

Bortole M (2011) Desenvolvimento de um Sensor Híbrido para Aplicações em Robótica e Fisioterapia. PhD thesis, Federal University of Espirito Santo

Breazeal C, Brooks R (2004) Robot emotions: a functional perspective. In: Fellous J-M, Arbib MA (eds) Who needs emotions? The brain meets the robot, chapter 10. Oxford University Press, New York, pp 271–310

Brooke J (2013) SUS: a retrospective. J Usability Stud 8(2):29–40

Cabibihan J-J, Javed H, Ang M, Aljunied SM (2013) Why robots? A survey on the roles and benefits of social robots in the therapy of children with autism. Int J Soc Robot 5(4):593–618

Cook A, Meng M-H, Gu J, Howery K (2002) Development of a robotic device for facilitating learning by children who have severe disabilities. IEEE Trans Neural Syst Rehabil Eng 10(3):178–187

Deutsch JE, Borbely M, Filler J, Huhn K, Guarrera-Bowlby P (2008) Use of a low-cost, commercially available gaming console (Wii) for rehabilitation of an adolescent with cerebral palsy. Phys Ther 88(10):1196–1207

Duquette A, Michaud F, Mercier H (2008) Exploring the use of a mobile robot as an imitation agent with children with low-functioning autism. Auton Robot 24(2):147–157

Ekman P (1999) Basic emotions. In: Dalgleish T, Power MJ (eds) Handbook of cognition and emotion. John Wiley & Sons, Ltd., West Sussex, pp 45–60

Encarnação P, Alvarez L, Rios A, Maya C, Adams K, Cook A (2014) Using virtual robot-mediated play activities to assess cognitive skills. Disabil Rehabil Assist Technol 9(3):231–241

Fernandez R, Arthur B, Fleming R (2013) Effect of doll therapy in managing challenging behaviours in people with dementia: a systematic review protocol. JBI Database System Rev Implement Rep 11(9):120–132

Fontes CMB, Mondini CCdSD, Moraes MCAF, Bachega MI, Maximino NP (2010) Using therapeutic toys in care with hospitalized children. Revista Brasileira de Educação Especial 16(1):95–106

François D, Powell S, Dautenhahn K (2009) A long-term study of children with autism playing with a robotic pet: taking inspirations from non-directive play therapy to encourage children's proactivity and initiative-taking. Interact Stud 10(3):324–373

Gatica-Rojas V, Méndez-Rebolledo G (2014) Virtual reality interface devices in the reorganization of neural networks in the brain of patients with neurological diseases. Neural Regen Res 9(8):888–896

Giannopulu I, Pradel G (2010) Multimodal interactions in free game play of children with autism and a mobile toy robot. NeuroRehabilitation 27(4):305–311

Giullian N, Ricks D, Atherton A, Colton M, Goodrich M, Brinton B (2010) Detailed requirements for robots in autism therapy. In: 2010 IEEE international conference on systems, man and cybernetics. IEEE, pp 2595–2602

Golomb MR, McDonald BC, Warden SJ, Yonkman J, Saykin AJ, Shirley B, Huber M, Rabin B, AbdelBaky M, Nwosu ME, Barkat-Masih M, Burdea GC (2010) In-home virtual reality videogame telerehabilitation in adolescents with hemiplegic cerebral palsy. Arch Phys Med Rehabil 91(1):1–8.e1

Guyton AC, Hall JE (2006) Functional organization of the human body, and control of the "internal environment" cells as the living units of the body. In: Textbook of medical physiology, 11th edn. Elsevier Saunders, Philadelphia

Howcroft J, Klejman S, Fehlings D, Wright V, Zabjek K, Andrysek J, Biddiss E (2012) Active video game play in children With cerebral palsy: potential for physical activity promotion and rehabilitation therapies. Arch Phys Med Rehabil 93(8):1448–1456

Hsieh H-C (2008) Effects of ordinary and adaptive toys on pre-school children with developmental disabilities. Res Dev Disabil 29(5):459–466

Kim ES, Berkovits LD, Bernier EP, Leyzberg D, Shic F, Paul R, Scassellati B (2013) Social robots as embedded reinforcers of social behavior in children with autism. J Autism Dev Disord 43(5):1038–1049

Komendziński T, Mikołajewska E, Mikołajewski D, Dreszer J, Bałaj B (2016) Cognitive robots in the development and rehabilitation of children with developmental disorders. Bio-Algorithms Med-Syst 12(3):93–98

Kozima H, Michalowski MP, Nakagawa C (2009) Keepon. Int J Soc Robot 1(1):3–18

Krasny-Pacini A, Hiebel J, Pauly F, Godon S, Chevignard M (2013) Goal attainment scaling in rehabilitation: a literature-based update. Ann Phys Rehabil Med 56(3):212–230

Lewis JR, Sauro J (2009) The factor structure of the system usability scale. In: Kurosu M (ed) Human centered design, HCD 2009. Lecture notes in computer science, vol 5619. Springer, Berlin/Heidelberg

McDougall J, King G (2007) Goal attainment scaling: description, utility, and applications in pediatric therapy services, 2nd edn. Thames Valley Children's Centre, London

Michaud F, Clavet A (2001) RoboToy contest – designing mobile robotic toys for autistic children. In: Proceedings of the American society for engineering education (ASEE'01), pp 1–4

Palsbo SE, Hood-Szivek P (2012) Effect of robotic-assisted three-dimensional repetitive motion to improve hand motor function and control in children with handwriting deficits: a nonrandomized phase 2 device trial. Am J Occup Ther 66(6):682–690

Paron-Wildes AJ (2005) Sensory stimulation and autistic children. Implications 6(4):1–5

Pearson Y, Borenstein J (2013) The intervention of robot caregivers and the cultivation of children's capability to play. Sci Eng Ethics 19(1):123–137

POB Technology (2005) POB-Bot user's manual. POB Technology, Chassieu

Ray DC, Lee KR, Meany-Walen KK, Carlson SE, Carnes-Holt KL, Ware JN (2013) Use of toys in child-centered play therapy. Int J Play Ther 22(1):43–57

Robins B, Amirabdollahian F, Ji Z, Dautenhahn K (2010) Tactile interaction with a humanoid robot for children with autism: a case study analysis involving user requirements and results of an initial implementation. In: 19th international symposium in robot and human interactive communication. IEEE, pp 704–711

Scherzer AL (1990) Early diagnosis and therapy in cerebral palsy: a primer on infant developmental problems. Pediatric habilitation, vol 6. CRC Press, New York

Seligman MEP (1992) Helplessness: on depression, development, and death. Series of books in psychology. W.H. Freeman & Company, New York

Sposito AMP, de Montigny F, Sparapani VdC, de Lima RAG, Silva-Rodrigues FM, Pfeifer LI, Nascimento LC (2016) Puppets as a strategy for communication with Brazilian children with cancer. Nurs Health Sci 18(1):30–37

Thomas RM (1993) Comparing theories child development. Wadsworth Publishing Company, Belmont

Valadão CT, Goulart C, Rivera H, Caldeira E, Bastos Filho TF, Frizera-Neto A, Carelli R (2016) Analysis of the use of a robot to improve social skills in children with autism spectrum disorder. Res Biomed Eng 32(2):161–175

Wu YN, Wilcox B, Donoghue JP, Crisco JJ, Kerman KL (2012) The impact of massed practice on children with hemiplegic cerebral palsy: pilot study of home-based toy play therapy. J Med Biol Eng 32(5):331–342

Wuang Y-P, Chiang C-S, Su C-Y, Wang C-C (2011) Effectiveness of virtual reality using Wii gaming technology in children with down syndrome. Res Dev Disabil 32(1):312–321

You SH, Jang SH, Kim Y-H, Kwon Y-H, Barrow I, Hallett M (2005) Cortical reorganization induced by virtual reality therapy in a child with hemiparetic cerebral palsy. Dev Med Child Neurol 47(9):628–635

Towards a Privacy Rule Conceptual Model for Smart Toys

**Laura Rafferty, Patrick C. K. Hung, Marcelo Fantinato,
Sarajane Marques Peres, Farkhund Iqbal, Sy-Yen Kuo, and Shih-Chia Huang**

1 Introduction

A toy is an item or product intended for learning or play, which can have various benefits to childhood development. The modern toy industry is comprised of establishments primarily engaged in manufacturing dolls, toys and games. As such a substantial part of human development, toys have continued to maintain a presence in the daily lives of billions of individuals of all ages. While primitive toys included rocks and pinecones, they soon progressed into dolls, stuffed animals

L. Rafferty (✉)
Faculty of Business and IT, University of Ontario Institute of Technology, Oshawa, ON, Canada
e-mail: laura.rafferty@uoit.ca

P.C.K. Hung
Faculty of Business and IT, University of Ontario Institute of Technology, Oshawa, ON, Canada

Department of Electronic Engineering, National Taipei University of Technology, Taipei, Taiwan
e-mail: patrick.hung@uoit.ca

M. Fantinato • S.M. Peres
School of Arts, Sciences and Humanities, University of São Paulo, São Paulo, Brazil
e-mail: m.fantinato@usp.br; sarajane@usp.br

F. Iqbal
College of Technological Innovation, Zayed University, Dubai, UAE
e-mail: farkhund.iqbal@zu.ac.ae

S.-Y. Kuo
Department of Electrical Engineering, National Taiwan University, Taipei, Taiwan
e-mail: sykuo@ntu.edu.tw

S.-C. Huang
Department of Electronic Engineering, National Taipei University of Technology, Taipei, Taiwan
e-mail: schuang@ntut.edu.tw

© Springer International Publishing AG 2017   85
J.K.T. Tang, P.C.K. Hung (eds.), *Computing in Smart Toys*, International Series
on Computer Entertainment and Media Technology,
DOI 10.1007/978-3-319-62072-5_6

and trains. Traditionally, toys have been entirely autonomous and without any processing or networking capabilities to communicate with any other device. While a child user is engaged with a traditional toy, it will collect and store no personal data, and requireno reason for concern for a child's privacy. With the introduction of electronic toys with embedded systems, electronic toys can have sensory capabilities, and the ability to collect and store inputted data based on the user's interactions. This data is limited and used only for the interaction, often discarded immediately. An electronic toy has limited or no networking capability. Thus, privacy concerns are limited to nonexistent in this context. In the past few decades, electronic toys such as Speak & Spell, Tamagotchi, and Furby had become popular.

A smart toy has been defined as a device consisting of a physical toy component that connects to one or more toy computing services to facilitate gameplay in the cloud through networking and sensory technologies to enhance the functionality of a traditional toy (Ren 2015). A smart toy in this context can be effectively considered an Internet of Things (IoT) with Artificial Intelligence (AI) which can provide Augmented Reality (AR) experiences to users. Examples of these are Mattel's Hello Barbie and Cognitoys' Dino. Smart toys are able to gather data on the context of the user (e.g., time of day, location, weather, etc.) and provide personalized services based on this context data. However, the user may not be comfortable with the level of data that is collected and inferred on them.

There are three general properties of a smart toy: (1) pervasive – a smart toy may follow child through everyday activities; (2) social – social aspects and multiplayer are becoming a mandatory aspect of interactive smart toys in a one-to-one, one-to-many and many-to-many relations (Tath 2006); and (3) connected – smart toys may connect and communicate with other toys and services through networks. For example, Cognitoys' Dino can listen and answer questions raised by children by voice because the Dino connected to the IBM Watson's knowledge called Elemental Path's "friendgine", which is a child-friendly database at the backend. Some research studies found out that children have emotional interactions with dolls and stuffed toys in anthropomorphic design (Tanaka 2009). Some children even prefer to take the toy to the dinner table or make a bed for it next to the child's own (Plowman 2004). Many studies found that anthropomorphic toys such as a teddy bear or bunny serve a specific purpose, as children trusted such designs and felt at ease disclosing private information.

As a result, *Toy Computing* is a recently developing concept which transcends the traditional toy into a new area of computer research using services computing technologies (Hung 2015) . In this context, a toy is a physical embodiment artifact that acts as a child user interface for toy computing services in cloud. A smart toy can also capture child user's physical activity state (e.g., voice, walking, standing, running, etc.) and store personalized information (e.g., location, activity pattern, etc.) through camera, microphone, Global Positioning System (GPS), and various sensors such as facial recognition or sound detection. In 2015, a new invention called the "Google Toy," which is an internet-connected teddy bear and bunny, like an anthropomorphic device with speech and face recognition functions that will have the ability to control smart home appliances and devices at home. However, this toy has caused many criticisms from the media as people express concern about privacy breaching and safety issues by Google.

More specifically, the toy makers are confronted with the challenge of better understanding the consumer needs, concerns and exploring the possibility of adopting such data-collected smart toys to rich information interface in this emerging market. For example, many toy designers have been researching the balance between the level of private information a toy collected from a child and the level of personalized features the toy provided to the child. Referring to the direction of the United States Federal Trade Commission Children's Online Privacy Protection Act (COPPA) and the European Union Data Protection Directive (EUDPD), the definition of a child to be an individual under the age of 13 years old. In this paper, the first assumption is that children do not understand the concept of privacy and the children do not know how to protect themselves online, especially in a social media and cloud environment. The second assumption is that children may disclose private information to smart toys and not be aware of the possible consequences and liabilities.

Breaches of privacy can result in threats to the physical safety of the child user (Schell 2007). While the parents (or any legal guardians) of a child strive to ensure their child's physical and online safety and privacy, there is no common approach for these parents to control the information flow between their child and the smart toys they interact with (Xia 2015). As smart toys are able to collect a variety of data such as text, picture, video, sound, location, and sensing data, this makes the context far more complicated than many other smart devices in particular given that the subjects are mainly children in a physical and social environment. Parental control is a feature in a smart toy for the parents to restrict the content the children can provide to the toy. Though the toy industry has also issued regulations for toy safety, these regulations have no mention of privacy issues in this toy computing paradigm.

This paper presents a privacy rule conceptual model with the concepts of toy, mobile service, device, and guidance with related privacy entities: purpose, recipient, obligation, and retention for the toy computing environment. In this model, the parents/ legal guardians are the owners of their child's data which is collected on their child (the data subject) in according to COPPA and EUDPD. Parents provide consent through access rules which allow their child's data to be shared according to their preferences and privacy compliance. This paper is organized as follows. Sect. 2 discusses related works and Sect. 3 presents the conceptual model with related algorithms. Next, Sect. 4 discusses the model in a prototype interface with example scenarios. Sect. 5 concludes the paper with future works.

2 Related Work

Recently the topic of smart toy is gaining increasingly more public interest. For example, Yahoo Canada published a report called "Electronic toy maker VTech's zero accountability clause puts onus for hacks on parents" on February 12, 2016, which said: "the collection of data through toys and apps geared towards children presents a growing challenge. In Canada we have a very restrictive and well defined privacy act for the healthcare domain. In the toy industry, they see all those safeguards and guidelines and they only talk about the safety of a toy. Those guidelines have not caught up to the information collecting aspect." This report shows the public concerns on the toy safety and privacy issues in our society. However, there is limited research on this specific cross-disciplinary research topic in toy computing. For example, AlHarthy and Shawkat (AlHarthy 2013) discuss a security solution to protect the network data from unauthorized access from controlling unmanaged smart devices, but they do not provide a generic privacy rule conceptual model for this paradigm. Next, Armando et al. (2014) describe a technical approach to secure the smart device paradigm based on a given organization's security policy, but without discussing the privacy protection model from the perspective of users. Then, Peng et al. (2013) present threat detection and mitigation mechanisms on mobile devices in a prioritized defense deployment, but they do not cover a privacy rule model to tackle the requirements of accessing mobile services. Referring to the research works in IoT, Alqassem and Svetinovic (2014) describe the challenges to tackling IoT privacy and security requirements as follows: (1) it is difficult to determine what information should be protected, when to protect it, and to whom access should be granted/restricted; (2) IoT consists of diverse technologies and the integration of these technologies may lead to unknown risks; and (3) the changing nature of the environment plays an important role when dealing with the privacy and security vulnerabilities of the IoT. Though there is a lot of related research in security and privacy of IoT, there is no standardized model which focuses on smart toys in this paradigm. For example, Sun et al. (2014) proposes a personal privacy protection policy model based on homomorphism encryption in IoT, but there is no specific privacy rule design.

With all of this in mind, privacy is a growing concern among many users of mobile devices. While many users appreciate the value of targeted services in mobile devices, they still express concern over how their data is collected and managed without their knowledge. For example, Cherubini et al. (2011) identify privacy as a barrier to the adoption of mobile phone context services. Seventy percent of consumers say it is important to know exactly what personal information is being collected and shared (MEF 2013), while 92% of users expressed concern about applications collecting personal information without their consent (Futuresight 2011). Mobile applications have adapted countless services to better analyze context data and provide custom services that will bring the most value to a user based on what they are most likely to need. While allowing context data to be collected for services can prove to be of great benefit to users, there is an ongoing tradeoff between utility and privacy (Chakraborty 2013). In summary, smart toys which embrace sensory and networking capabilities open up new threats to privacy (Heurix 2015), stimulate new user requirements (Atamli 2014), and establish a unique case for privacy rule model in toy computing. To our best knowledge, there is still no legislation or industry standard which specifically regulates security and privacy requirements for smart toys.

For illustration, the conceptual model we discuss in this paper focuses on how to protect the child's location information based on IETF RFC6280. Referring to IETF RFC6280 by Barnes et al. (2011), Geopriv is an Internet Best Current Practice for location and location privacy in internet applications, which enables users to express preferences for the disclosure of their location information. For example, the user can make a rule that their location is not to be disclosed beyond the intended recipient. This architecture binds the privacy rules to the data so that receiving entities are informed of when their data is shared to other parties. Various techniques have been used in attempt to preserve the privacy of a user's location. Some approaches include degrading quality, creating fake location points, uncertainty, pseudonyms, sharing opaque identifiers using symmetric key encryption, k-anonymity through cloaking. Pseudonyms and k-anonymity methods have been proven inadequate for protecting users' location data and preventing re-identification.

On the other hand, location-based services, also known as location-aware mobile services, have become widely popular to provide information such as events, traveling, shopping and entertainment. Location-based services have been defined by Duri et al. (2001) as "services in which the location of a person or an object is used to shape or focus the application or service". Pura (2005) identifies location as one of the most promising applications of mobile commerce, due to the ability to allow service providers to offer customized services based on context and resulting in increased perceived value and loyalty of customers.

The mobile application industry has observed a widespread adoption of mobile game applications such as Pokemon Go (Niantic 2016). This has been successful due to factors such as increased mobility and social network integration (Baber 2004). Location-based services have also been used in applications for games. The popular mobile game Angry Birds (Rovio 2015) has a location-based feature which allows users to compete with other based on a leader board associated with their location. Next, MyTown (Booyah 2015.) is another mobile game, reminiscent of Monopoly, where users can check in to a physical location, buy and sell properties, and collect rent from other players who check into the same location. Then, Kaasinen (2003) conducted a study to investigate user needs for location-aware mobile services:

- **Contents**: topical up to date information, comprehensive relevant information, interaction (user is moving and can only provide limited interaction to device), push information based on both location and personalization, detailed search options, planning vs. spontaneity.
- **Personalization**: personal options and contents, user-generated content.
- **Seamless service entities**: consistency, seamless solutions to support the whole user activity.

- **Privacy**: the right to locate, use, store, and forward the location. Privacy requirements are based on legislation and social regulation. The paper also identifies
Platform for Privacy Preferences (P3P) (Wenning 2007) as a potential approach
to manage user privacy preferences and compare them to the location-aware
service's privacy practices. P3P is a privacy policy framework created by the
World Wide Web Consortium (W3C), based on the eXtensible Markup Language
(XML), designed to help end users manage their privacy while navigating
websites that have differing privacy policies. User's privacy preferences are
expressed using A P3P Preference Exchange Language (APPEL), which enables
websites to express their privacy practices in a standard format that can be
retrieved automatically and interpreted easily by users of P3P browsers. We also
adopt the concepts built in P3P into our conceptual model.

3   Privacy Rule Conceptual Model

Privacy rules can be achieved through privacy preserving mechanisms such as
access control. In order to provide the most relevant content, the smart toy will
need to collect certain context data such as the child's location, and also potential
profile information such as age and gender to help determine what their interests
may be based on demographic. To gain even more context of the child, the smart
toy may collect and retain historical data on the child such as previous movement
patterns via GPS, camera and various sensors, to determine where the child is likely
to be at certain times, if the child is travelling, or previous interactions with the
smart toy such as which content they had previously been interested in. It is clear
that the more information is collected on the child, the more relevant services can
be provided to the child. However, the user may not be comfortable with the level
of data that is collected and inferred on them (Shen 2015). There are countless
types of data that can be collected from smart toys that must be considered when
evaluating the scope of privacy. This is true of collected sensory data, and also from
within other applications, sensitive data can be collected such as a user's profile
information, contact list, or calendar. All of this information can be collected and
analyzed to determine context data about the children and then the smart toy may
provide personalized functions (Fu 2015).

Referring to Fig. 1, the children (users) may interact with different smart toys
from different toy makers in a physical and social environment such as Mattel's
Hello Barbie and Cognitoys' Dino. The smart toys may be equipped with camera,
microphone, GPS, and sensors for face and sound detection. These smart toys
may send the collected information such as text, picture, video, sound (voice),
location and sensing data to the toy computing services, which are published and
managed by different toy computing providers and even bind with other third party
services, in the cloud. Each smart toy should have its own privacy policy that
outlines information including how it will collect, manage, share, and retain the
user's personal data (Fu 2015).

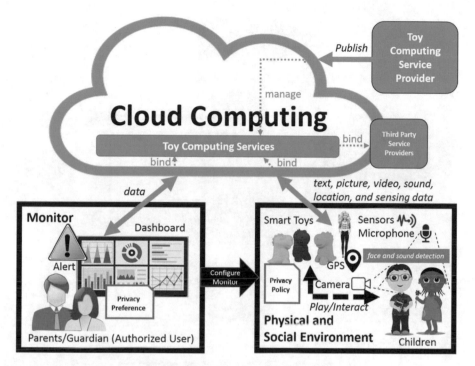

Fig. 1 Conceptual model of toy computing

In the privacy rule conceptual model, a subject is a *3-tuple* entity comprised of a smart toy, a device, and a mobile service. The mobile service may communicate with external entities over a network, such as other devices or cloud services. The user who interacts with the subject is a child (data subject) who is associated with an identity and a parent (data owner) who is in control of their data. In this model, access control decisions are based on permissions which are assigned by the parent, comprised of a list of rules for operations (read, write, etc.) and objects. Fig. 2 illustrates a core access control model which allows parents to manage their privacy preferences for access to their child's location data, as an illustrative example. In the toy computing environment, location data is particularly sensitive data because it is the location of the child using the toy. The location object is sensitive information when associated with the user's identity since it allows other entities to be aware of the child's physical location. The motivation for this access control model is to protect this property from being shared with untrusted external entities. The motivation for this access control model is to protect this property from being shared with untrusted external entities.

Traditional access control models make access decisions (permit/deny) based on low level operations, such as read and write, for describing a subject's operation on an object. For example, user *A* is allowed to read file *B*, in which case user *A* is the subject, file *B* is the object, and read is the operation. Figure 3 presents an extended access control model for privacy in a toy computing environment.

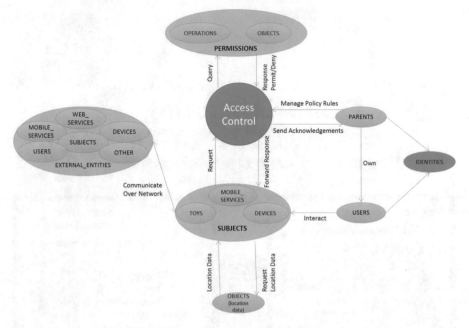

Fig. 2 Core access control model

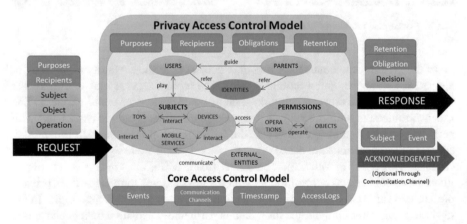

Fig. 3 Extended privacy access control model

This model shows the privacy access control model extended over top of the core access control model discussed in Fig. 2. In the privacy access control model, a request *<Subject, Operation, Object, Purposes, Recipients>* as input, and a response *<Decision, Obligations, Retentions>* as output, as well as an optional acknowledgement *<Subject, Event>* through a communication channel.

In the privacy rule conceptual model, a subject is a *3-tuple* entity comprised of a smart toy, a device, and a mobile service. The mobile service may communicate with external entities over a network, such as other devices or cloud services. The user who interacts with the subject is a child (data subject) who is associated with an identity and a parent (data owner) who is in control of their data. In this model, access control decisions are based on permissions which are assigned by the parent, comprised of a list of rules for operations (read, write, etc.) and objects. Figure 2 illustrates a core access control model which allows parents to manage their privacy preferences for access to their child's location data, as an illustrative example. In the toy computing environment, location data is particularly sensitive data because it is the location of the child using the toy. The location object is sensitive information when associated with the user's identity since it allows other entities to be aware of the child's physical location. The motivation for this access control model is to protect this property from being shared with untrusted external entities. The motivation for this access control model is to protect this property from being shared with untrusted external entities.

Traditional access control models make access decisions (permit/deny) based on low level operations, such as read and write, for describing a subject's operation on an object. For example, user A is allowed to read file B, in which case user A is the subject, file B is the object, and read is the operation. Figure 3 presents an extended access control model for privacy in a toy computing environment. This model shows the privacy access control model extended over top of the core access control model discussed in Fig. 2. In the privacy access control model, a request *<Subject, Operation, Object, Purposes, Recipients>* as input, and a response *<Decision, Obligations, Retentions>* as output, as well as an optional acknowledgement *<Subject, Event>* through a communication channel.

In our extension for preserving privacy, we have proposed four privacy-based entities: PURPOSES, RECIPIENTS, OBLIGATIONS and RETENTIONS based on P3P into the model (Wenning 2007) describedas follows:

- **PURPOSES:** is a set of purposes in the system. A subject must specify a set of purposes in the corresponding access request. A purpose can be described as different sub-purposes or combined into a general purpose in a hierarchical structure (He 2003). Figure 4 shows an illustrative hierarchical structure to represent purposes that could be related to toy computing. Different purposes can be generalized as the root element "AnyPurpose", which is the most general purpose in the system. "AnyPurpose" can be subclassified as "Personal Purpose", "MarketingPurpose", "Administrative Purpose", "GamePurpose" and "ResearchPurpose". Each of these can further be subclassified into more specific purposes.

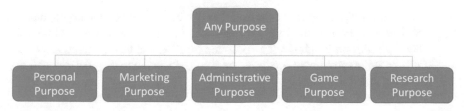

Fig. 4 Illustrative purpose hierarchy structure

- **RECIPIENTS:** is a set of recipients of the collected object(s) belonging to the subjects/users in the system. Each collected object has a corresponding set of recipients. In the context of toy computing and P3P, recipients can be described as one of the following categories:

    (a) *Individual:* the subject who made the request or an individual in the system.
    (b) *Group:* a group of users (e.g., the group of USERS or SUBJECTS currently engaged in a toy computing game session).
    (c) *Third-party*: an entity which does not belong to the system, but is constrained by and accountable to the object owner. This includes EXTERNAL_ENTITIES in Fig. 3.
    (d) *Anyone:* any subject or external entity.

- **OBLIGATIONS:** is a set of obligations in the system that is necessary to be accepted after access permission is granted. The obligations describe the rules that a subject agrees to comply with after gaining the access permission. Obligations are generally bound to legislation and agreements (e.g., "No disclosure to an unauthorized third party").

- **RETENTIONS:** is a set of retention policies in the system to be enforced after permission is granted. Each object may have a corresponding retention policy to enforce the duration for how long it may be used or retained. It is recommended that a child's location data be retained only for the time necessary for the stated purpose. Based on the context of P3P, the retention policy can be described as one of the following categories:

    (a) *No-retention:* the requested object is not retained for more than a brief period of time, after which it must be destroyed without being logged, archived or stored by the recipients.
    (b) *Stated-purpose*: the requested object is retained for the time required to meet the stated purpose and will be discarded as soon as possible after the purpose is satisfied.
    (c) *Legal-requirement:* the requested object is retained to meet a stated purpose (as required by law or liability under applicable law).
    (d) *Business-practices:* the requested object is retained under the stated business practices.
    (e) *Indefinitely*: the requested object is retained for an indeterminate period of time.

While we are concerned with location data, some relevant categories are shown in Fig. 5 as follows:

(a) *AnyLocationObjectType*: is a general description of any location object type.
(b) *Absolute Location*: is the location expressed in a range or exact GPS coordinates, latitude and longitude. The absolute location can be expressed as coarse (GPS-based, approximate location) or fine (network-based, precise location) (Android 2015).

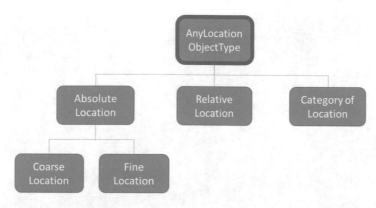

Fig. 5 Location object types

(c) **Relative Location**: is the location relative to another entity as a reference point. Relative location can be expressed as the distance between user A and user B, user A and device C, or user A and location D.

(d) **Categotical Location**: is the location expressed in a predefined category. Some examples include home, office, street, mall, or restaurant.

Referring to Fig. 3, a subject has access to an object, only if the access is authorized by the core access control. Also, the subject needs to specify the purposes of the access and the recipients of the result of the access operation. The purposes and the recipients must be legitimated according to the access of the object defined by the owner or an authority such as the government. Thus, obligations and a retention policy will be returned as a response message if the access is allowed. The subject must also comply with the obligations and the retention policies. The access request will be denied otherwise.

Parents can create policy rules for their child's data through the process illustrated in Fig. 6. This process is done through a mobile Web interface on the mobile device. The policy rule creation process starts with the initialization phase, whose first step is for the parent to configure themselves as the child (user)'s parent. By mapping a parent to a child user, the parent becomes the owner of the child's data. Next, the parent consents to the End User License Agreement (EULA) on behalf of the child, agreeing to the terms of the mobile service. Lastly, the parent sets their communication channel (e.g., email address) and preferences for receiving acknowledgements of privacy updates related to their child's data. As the second step, the parent can create policy rules according to their preferences for how their child's data can be collected and shared. This model uses positive authorization, in which parents define the rules for what is allowed. To create a policy rule, the parent first specifies the subject (their child), the object (e.g., absolute location data), the allowed operation (e.g., read), the allowed purposes (e.g., game purpose), and the allowed recipients (e.g., other users in-game). Next, the parent specifiesthe

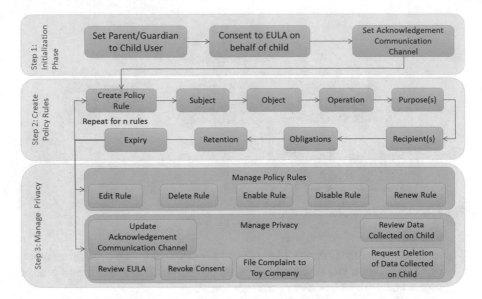

Fig. 6 Privacy rule creation process

obligations and retention policies that the recipient must comply to in order to receive the data object with an expiry date. After a rule is created, this second step can be repeated to create as many rules as desired. Step 3 shows the administrative tasks to manage the privacy rules.

The access control decision procedure in the privacy access control model is described in Fig. 7. A subject first requests access to a user's location information, specifying the subject, object, operation, purposes, and recipients. After receiving the request, as the second step, the privacy access control model processes the request as follows: (1) checks the owner of the requested object; (2) retrieves the corresponding privacy rules from the system; and, then, (3) checks the acknowledgment communication channel for the subject owner. Next, as the third step, the decision is made by: (1) checking the permissions from the core access control model; (2) checking the allowed purposes; and, then, (3) checking allowed recipients. As the fourth step, the final decision is made and the system returns a response and acknowledgement. The response can be either permit, along with the obligations and retention policy or deny. If applicable, the acknowledgement is sent to the subject owner through the predefined acknowledgement channel, and contains the subject and event. Lastly, the model records all of the above in the audit logs.

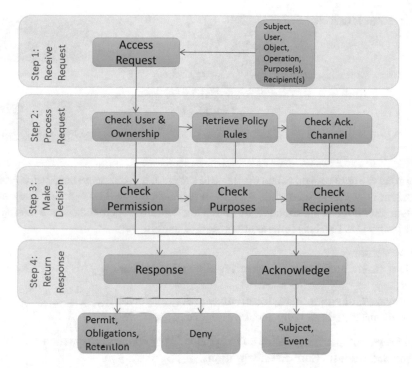

Fig. 7 Access control decision process

4 Discussion

Referring to a toy computing scenario, in this section we present some example scenarios using Tek Recon, and Sphero to illustrate some possible privacy access control rules based on the model.

Scenario 1 Sphero (2014) is another recent toy computing product in the industry, first introduced in 2011 by Orbotix, which then released subsequent versions, Sphero 2.0 in 2013 and Sphero Ollie in 2014. Referring to Fig. 8, Sphero is a robotic ball which can be controlled and programmed through the user's smartphone or tablet. There are over 30 apps available for Sphero, most of which are games, while others are focused on education. This product is marketed not only to children and can be appropriate for any age group. While the physical ball component is a very simple and traditional concept, the capabilities of the toy increase substantially with the inclusion of robotics and a mobile device. The Sphero ball has wireless networking capabilities, an accelerometer and gyroscope, rolls in every direction, and glows different and a mobile device. The Sphero ball has wireless networking capabilities, an accelerometer and gyroscope, rolls in every direction, and glows different colors. Sphero can be programmed by the user through an app called Sphero Macrolab, which includes a set of predefined macros, and more advanced

Fig. 8 Example scenario 1:
Sphero

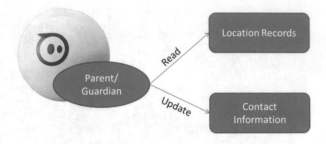

users can use another app called orbBasic to program in a language based on BASIC. A parent may access their child's location records collected by Sphero. They may update their contact information for receiving acknowledgements. Some examples of privacy rules for this scenario are presented as follows.

Privacy Rules

S1.1: A parent/guardian (data owner) is allowed to read or copy his child's location record.

   (Parent/Guardian, read, locationRecord, _, _, permit, _, _)
   (Parent/Guardian, copy, locationRecord, _, _, permit, _, _)

S1.2: A parent/guardian is allowed to update his/her contact information
   (owner, update, ContactInformation, _, _, permit, _, _)

Scenario 2 Tek Recon (Tech4Kids 2013.): is a line of toy blasters developed by Tech4Kids, marketed to children aged 8 years and up in 2013. While this product features a physical component identical in concept to a traditional toy blaster, the novelty is the ability to integrate with a mobile device. Referring to Fig. 9, the Tek Recon blaster features a mount on top where a smartphone is inserted. A mobile application has been developed by Tech4Kids which operates in collaboration with the physical blaster to augment traditional blaster-based games. The application provides several functionalities including a scope, which uses the smartphone camera to display what is in front of the user with additional features overlaid on top, such as ammunition, score, radio, and a GPS location map of other players. The application has networking functionality to create and join games with friends over a LAN or mobile network. The user is also required to create an account online, where the scores and account information are stored. As shown in Fig. 9, a child using Tek Recon has been connected to a mobile service using location services in a toy computing environment to share his location to their friends and see their locations in return. Once the service receives the user's location record, the service may read and disclose the location information to other players for the purpose of the game, and delete the records immediately after the game is complete. An example of privacy rule for this scenario 2 is presented as follows.

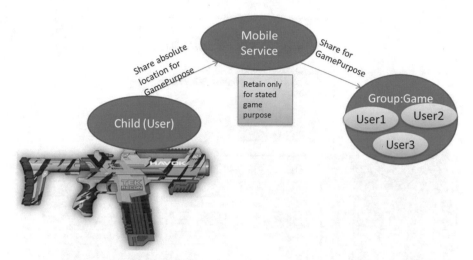

Fig. 9 Example scenario 2: Tek Recon

Privacy Rule

S2.1. A service is allowed to read the absolute location record of a user for the purpose of a game if and only if the service follows obligations of disclosure to group "game" and not to keep the record after stated game purpose has ended.

(MobileService, read, Absolute_Location, GamePurpose, Group:Game, permit, _, StatedPurpose)

Referring to Fig. 10, we present a demo of an interface for parents to use in an initial setup to configure preferences and create policy rules. These options would appear during initial setup of a toy computing application. These privacy settings allow parents to create access control rules based on their preferences on concepts from P3P, i.e. purposes, recipients, obligations, and retentions. The first step in the configuration process is the Profile Setup phase. The Profile Setup phase includes three sections, the Parent Contact Details, Child Information, and Privacy Policy Review. The parent enters their basic information including name and email address, and then selects if they wish to receive email updates on their child's privacy-related information. Next, on the Child Information page, the child's first name is entered for management purposes, and the parent then agrees to take ownership over their child's data. Next, the privacy policy of the toy application is presented to the parent to review. The parent reviews the policy and must confirm that they have read and agree to the terms before proceeding. By agreeing to the terms, the parent is providing consent on their child's behalf.

The next phase is the Privacy Rule creation phase, when the parent is able to create one or more privacy rules for how their child's private location data is used. By default, there is no policy rules yet configured. A new rule can be created or a template can be used. Templates of useful policy rules can be provided to simplify

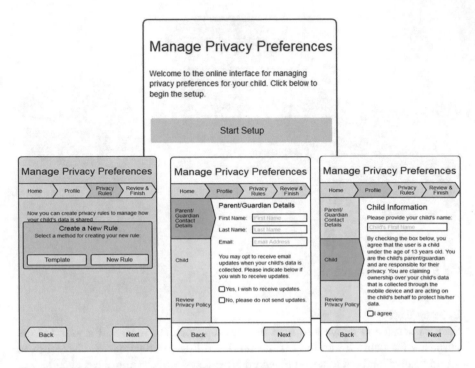

Fig. 10 Prototype interface demonstration

the rule configuration process for parents. The first step of creating a new privacy rule is the General Settings. In the General Settings, the parent can name the rule, provide a description, and set an expiry date for how long the rule will be in effect. Next, in the Core Access Control settings, the mobile service (subject), location resource (object), and operation are selected. The objects selected are the absolute location and relative location. Next, the settings for Purposes and Recipients are also presented. The parent chooses from a list of purposes they wish to accept, as well as a list of types of recipients. The types of recipients can be expanded to be more specific, such as Third-Party: Marketing, or Group: Game Players.

The next steps are the Obligations and Retention settings, and then finally reviewing and adding the rule, as shown in Fig. 10, the parent first selects the obligations that the service must comply with upon receiving the child's data. Obligations can include compliance with PIPEDA or COPPA. The parent can also search from a list of other obligations, or input a custom obligation policy. For retention, the parent can select how long they wish to allow their child's data to be retained. Finally, on the Review & Add Rule page, the privacy rule is presented in plain English. Once the parent reviews the rule, they can select "Confirm and Add Rule" at the bottom of the screen. Once a privacy rule is added, the parent is directed to the Manage Privacy Rules page, which shows a table of all of the configured privacy rules and their status (e.g., enabled, disabled, or expired). This provides options to enable, disable, edit, delete, or create new rules. A parent can also return to this screen at a later time to manage rules or renew expired rules. Once the parent is satisfied with the privacy rules, he/she can select "Next" to be directed to the final Review & Finish page. This page summarizes all of the settings and confirms that the parent has completed all of the sections. A list of enabled privacy rules and their corresponding expiry dates is also presented. Finally, the parent can select "Save and Finish" to save their settings and finish the setup. Then the settings will take effect immediately.

5 Conclusions

This paper presented a privacy rule conceptual model for smart toys which is one of the first attempts in this emerging research topic. The model allows parents to create privacy rules and receive acknowledgements regarding their child's privacy sensitive location data. Next, we presented the algorithm for access control decisions for privacy enforcement, and finally we illustrated the applicability of the privacy rules in a practical environment using example scenarios with popular toy computing toys in the industry. We are currently conducting an empirical study to justify the user acceptability of the prototype interface for the privacy rule conceptual model.

Acknowledgements This work was supported by the São Paulo Research Foundation (Fapesp) under Grants 2015/16615-0 and 2016/00014-0. This work was also supported by the Research Office - Zayed University, Abu Dhabi, United Arab Emirates, under Research Projects: R15048 & R16083; by the Ministry of Science and Technology (MOST), Taiwan, under MOST Grants: 105-2923-E-002 -014 -MY3, 105-2923-E-027 -001 -MY3, 105-2221-E-027 -113, & 105-2811-E-027 -001; and the Natural Sciences and Engineering Research Council of Canada (NSERC), under Discovery Grants Program: RGPIN-2016-05023.

References

AlHarthy KA (2013) Implement network security control solutions in BYOD environment. The 2013 IEEE International Conference on Control System, Computing and Engineering (ICCSCE). IEEE, Batu Ferringhi, pp 7–11

Alqassem IA (2014) A taxonomy of security and privacy requirements for the Internet of Things (IoT). The IEEE International Conference on Industrial Eng. and Engineering Management. IEEE, Malaysia, pp 1244–1248

Android (2015). Location strategies, Android Developer. http://developer.android.com/guide/topics/location/strategies.html.

Armando AC (2014) Securing the bring your own device paradigm. Computer 47(6):48–56

Atamli AA (2014) Threat-based security analysis for the internet of things. The 2014 International Workshop on Secure Internet of Things. IEEE, Oslo, pp 35–43

Baber CA (2004) Social networks and mobile games: the use of bluetooth for a multiplayer card game. The 6th International Conference on Human Computer Interaction with Mobile Devices and Services. Glasgow.

Barnes RL (2011) An architecture for location and location Privacy in internet applications. Internet Engineering Task Force (IETF), https://tools.ietf.org/html/rfc6280

Booyah (2015) iTunes – MyTown2. https://itunes.apple.com/app/mytown-2/id442345455

Chakraborty SR (2013) A framework for context-aware privacy of sensor data on mobile systems. In: The fourteenth workshop on Mobile Computing Systems and Applications (ACM HotMobile2013). ACM, New York

Cherubini MD (2011) Barriers and bridges in the adoption of today's mobile phone contextual services. In: MobileHCI '11. ACM, Stockholm

Duri SC (2001) An approach to providing a seamless end-user experience for location-aware applications. The 1st International Workshop on Mobile Commerce 86(4):20

Fu ZR (2015) Enabling personalized search over encrypted outsourced data with efficiency improvement. IEEE Trans Parallel Distri Syst

Futuresight (2011) User Perspectives on Mobile Privacy – Summary of Research Findings. GSMA 27(9):2546–2559

He Q (2003) Privacy enforcement with an extended role-based access control model. NCSU Computer Science Technical Report TR-2003-09. ACM, Raleigh

Heurix JZ (2015) A taxonomy for privacy enhancing technologies. Comput Secur 53:1–17

Hung PC (2015) Mobile services for toy computing, the Springer International Series on Applications and Trends in Computer Science. Springer International Publishing, Switzerland

Kaasinen E (2003) User needs for location-aware mobile services. Pers Ubiquit Comput 7(1):70–79

MEF (2013) MEF global privacy report 2013. MEF, http://www.mefmobile.org/

Niantic I (2016) Pokemon Go. http://www.pokemongo.com/

Peng WL (2013) T-dominance: prioritized defense deployment for BYOD security. The 2013 IEEE Conference on Communications and Network Security (CNS), USA. pp 37–45

Plowman LA (2004) Interactivity, interfaces, and smart toys. Computer 37(2):98–100

Pura M (2005) Linking perceived value and loyalty in location-based mobile services. Manag Serv Qual 15(6):509–538

Ren YS (2015) Mutual verifiable provable data auditing in public cloud storage. J Internet Tech 16(2):317–323

Rovio (2015) Angry birds www.rovio.com/en/our-work/games/view/1/angry-birds

Schell BH (2007) Cyber child pornography: a review paper of the sand legal issues and remedies, aggression and violent behavior. Elsevier 12(1):45–63

Shen JM (2015) Enhanced secure sensor association and key management in wireless body area networks. J Commun Netw 17(5):453–462

Sphero (2014) Sphero. http://www.gosphero.com

Sun GH (2014) A privacy protection policy combined with privacy homomorphism in the internet of things. The 23rd International Conference on Computer Communication and Networks (ICCCN), Shanghai, pp 1–6

Tanaka FA (2009) The use of robots in early education: a scenario based on ethical consideration. The 18th IEEE international symposium on robot and human interactive communication, Toyama, pp 558–560

Tath EI (2006) Context data model for privacy. PRIME Standardization Workshop IBM Zurich, Zurich, 6 Pages

Tech4Kids (2013) Tek Recon-Tech4Kids. http://www.tekrecon.com/

Wenning R (2007) Platform for Privacy Preferences (P3P) project: enabling smarter privacy tools for the web. http://www.w3.org/P3P

Xia ZW (2015) A secure and dynamic multi-keyword ranked search scheme over encrypted cloud data. IEEE Trans Parallel Distrib Syst 27(2):340–352

Designing for Parental Control: Enriching Usability and Accessibility in the Context of Smart Toys

André de Lima Salgado, Leandro Agostini do Amaral, Paula Costa Castro, and Renata Pontin de Mattos Fortes

1 Parental Control Interfaces for Smart Toys

Parental Control interface is integrated within smart toys as a measure of addressing privacy concerns by parents. Rafferty et al. (2015) argued that Parental Control is one of the key features to deal with children's privacy issues in toy computing. The intent is to simulate the real world control parent have in day to day activities and interaction their children have in the real world within Smart Toys world. In consequence, Parental Control is a strategy to deal with privacy problems that may occur while children play with Smart Toys, when their privacy may be exposed for different reasons. In these situations, parents want to ensure privacy and security of their children's data. For this reason, Parental Control solutions are necessary in complement to Smart Toy support and settings applications.

In this context, diverse Smart Toys in the industry have implemented Parental Control settings among their applications. The CogniToys Dino[1], at the time of this writing, has indicated the development of a "Parent Panel". Similarly, Jibo Privacy Statement[2] provides parents with privacy details about their children using the toy in

---

[1] CogniToys Dino website at: https://cognitoys.com/. Accessed Jun 28th, 2017.

[2] Jibo website: https://www.jibo.com/privacy. Accessed Jun 28th, 2017.

A. de Lima Salgado (✉) • L.A. do Amaral • R.P. de Mattos Fortes
Institute of Mathematical Science and Computing, University of São Paulo (USP),
São Carlos, SP, Brazil
e-mail: alsalgado@usp.br; leandroagostini@usp.br; renata@icmc.usp.br

P.C. Castro
Department of Gerontology, Federal University of São Carlos (UFSCAR), São Carlos, SP, Brazil
e-mail: castro@ufscar.br

© Springer International Publishing AG 2017
J.K.T. Tang, P.C.K. Hung (eds.), *Computing in Smart Toys*, International Series on Computer Entertainment and Media Technology,
DOI 10.1007/978-3-319-62072-5_7

103

order to request their consent and permission. In addition, the Hello Barbie App[3] has "Safety & Privacy" settings requesting parents' consent for their children using the Hello Barbie toy. The limitations of current interfaces for parental control include poor usability and lack of options for fine-tuning of privacy preferences. Figure 1 shows examples of common parental control interfaces[4], as privacy policies and profile setup, based on Rafferty et al. (2015) recommendations to overcome these limitations.

According to the European Union Safer Internet Program (n.d.), the following parameters are considered as core in the development of Parental Control interfaces: *functionality*, *effectiveness*, *usability* and *security*. The European Union Safer Internet Program showed *functionality*, as well as effectiveness, are considered components of usability (ISO/IEC 25066 2016; ISO 9241-161 2016). Thus, usability is, along with security, an important attribute for Parental Control interfaces.

Besides the importance of developing usable Parental Controls, Chin et al. (2012) showed evidence that may indicate that user experience with sensitive applications (such as Parental Control) might be still weakened by users' discomfort. Similarly, Liu et al. (2014) argued that different studies in the literature indicate that the permission granting process is still confusing for users, which may have caused a negative influence on users' satisfaction. Additionally, Liu et al. (2016) argued *"users are often unaware of, if not uncomfortable with, many of their permission settings"*. In such cases, users' comfort impact their satisfaction and, in consequence, the usability of the interface (ISO/IEC 25066 2016; ISO 9241-161 2016).

In this context, usability remains a challenge in the development of Parental Control for new technologies, such as Smart Toys. Tang and Tewell (2015) reviewed emerging technologies for toy Human-Toy Interaction, but methods for development of usable and accessible interfaces for Parental Control were not approached. Also, the literature shows that a correct balance between usability, security and privacy is a design challenge (Dhillon et al. 2016; Alshamari 2016). Because security and privacy are key aspects of Parental Control interfaces, we aimed to compose a guide for security and privacy professionals to help them in the development of more usable Parental Control interfaces for Smart Toys.

This chapter is a review of traditional HCI (Human-Computer Interaction) methods, with examples focused on Parental Control interfaces in the context of Smart Toys, aiming practitioners from security and privacy area. In addition, we presented a discussion on future trends for Smart Toys focusing on a highly important need: development of technologies for elderly healthcare.

---

[3]Hello Barbie website: https://www.toytalk.com/product/hello-barbie/.

[4]Designed using Material Design guidelines and free icons from: https://material.google.com/style/icons.html#icons-product-icons.

Fig. 1 Examples of Parental Control interfaces, designed from the recommendations of Rafferty et al. (2015)

2 Terms and Definitions

This section presents definitions for important terms related to design of interfaces, and the design of Parental Control interfaces in particular. Thus, we described the following terms: user experience (UX), usability and accessibility. These terms were described according to international standards and recent studies.

2.1 User Experience (UX)

A unified definition of User Experience (UX) is still under discussion in the specialized literature, while the term is already popular in market and industry. Some authors have contributed towards initial unified definition for the term. Previous studies showed that UX might involve users' feelings as well as affective and hedonic aspects related to their interactions with interfaces (Law et al. 2009; Hartson and Pyla 2012). In sequence, the ISO ISO/IEC 25066 provided an important contribution towards a wide accepted definition, as shown below:

> *User Experience (UX)* is *"a person's perceptions and responses that result from the use and/or anticipated use of a product, system or service".*

According to the ISO/IEC 25066, UX includes users' emotions and is related to the usability and assistive capabilities of an interactive product. In consequence, it is related to these terms, usability and accessibility. The following sections present definitions for both terms.

2.2 Usability and Accessibility

Usability is one of the important factors that can impact the quality and ergonomics of a software interface (ISO 9241-210 2010; ISO/IEC 25066 2016). The ISO/IEC 25066 (2016) presented the usability definition as follows:

> *Usability* is the *"extent to which a system, product or service can be used by specified users to achieve specified goals with effectiveness, efficiency and satisfaction in a specified context of use".*

In situations that users have the widest range of capabilities, the ISO 9241-161 (2016b) considered usability as a synonym of accessibility. In this context, accessibility could also be considered as a component of UX, and important to the design of Parental Control interfaces. Nonetheless, a unified definition for accessibility is still under discussion in the literature of the field. In this context, Petrie et al. (2015) have suggested a unified definition for accessibility of Web technologies. For Petrie et al. (Petrie et al. 2015), accessibility of Web interfaces refers to the extent to which any user (disabled and older users in particular) can interact with an interface in different contexts of use with usability. The definition for accessibility provided by the ISO 9241-161 (2016b) is as follows:

> **Accessibility** is *"usability of a product, service, environment or facility by people with the widest range of capabilities"*.

At this point, we have presented three major terms related to quality and ergonomics of Parental Control interfaces. However, the process of developing these characteristics for such interfaces still must be discussed. For this reason, the following section presents content for the entire design process, User Centered Design, understood in the area of Human-Computer Interaction as fundamental for development of UX, usability and accessibility of interfaces.

3   User-Centered Design (UCD)

The term User-Centered Design (UCD) is often shown as a synonym of a wider term, Human-Centered Design (HCD). In the scenario of UCD, people that interact with the interface can be considered (act) as users, and not the broader term "Human" (ISO 9241–210 2010). UCD process was described in the Human-Computer Interaction (HCI) literature as a fundamental process of design for the development of usable interfaces (Katzeff et al. 2012; Norman 2013; Preece et al. 2015).

ISO 9241 series showed that the UCD process approaches development and design of interactive systems in order to make them more usable, by applying human factors/ergonomics and usability techniques (ISO 9241-210 2010). Since the study of Gould and Lewis (1985), the UCD approach has been based on three principles (Katzeff et al. 2012; Preece et al. 2015), as described in sequence:

- **Early focus on users and Tasks:** understanding who the users are, their characteristics (e.g. cognitive and behavioral) and the nature of their work (e.g. how it is accomplished by tasks).
- **Empirical Measurement:** observe real users using the product (or a prototype), observing and analyzing their performance and reactions.
- **Iterative Design:** the UCD must be a cycle. When problems are discovered from the evaluation activities, they may be corrected in a sequential cycle.

As reinforced in the principle *Interactive Design*, UCD process is a sequential cycle. Based on the ISO 9241–210 definition for HCD, which can be applied for those cases when Humans can be considered just users of the interface, UCD can be defined as follows:

User Centered Design (UCD) is the development and design of interfaces in order to make them more usable based on it their use, applying human factors/ergonomics and usability techniques.

Usually, a common UCD cycle encompasses the following stages: Requirements Analysis, (Re)Design, Prototype and Evaluation (Preece et al. 2015). The UCD process normally starts by establishing new requirements from users' needs. These requirements can be obtained from both an initial requirement analysis – after the identification of a need – or from outcomes from an evaluation stage – belonging to a previous UCD cycle. The following sections show each of the phases of the UCD process.

3.1   Requirements Analysis

Requirements Analysis can occur at the beginning of a UCD process, or also at a subsequent cycle, after a previous *Evaluation* stage. In the initial Requirements Analysis – just after the identification of a need – questionnaires with users and/or interviews with experts (may be usability or application domain experts) take place. These techniques can help organizations to collect important and fundamental information for the whole process of interface development. In many cases, these techniques provide the initial information about users' characteristics (Preece et al. 2015).

Further information about user characteristics can be found via task analysis techniques. These techniques allow practitioners to understand important aspects related to usability and accessibility, such as how users perform specific sequence of actions in order to complete a task and achieve their goal. A common technique for task analysis is the Hierarchical Task Analysis (HTA), which allows practitioners to represent actions of a user task by structuring it on a real representative hierarchy. HTA can also be used to understand differences between how the users perform their tasks in a real situation (based on users' mental models[5]) with the interface in order to achieve a specific goal (Dix et al. 2003; Norman 2013; Preece et al. 2015). Mental models can be understood as representations, in the user's mind, of how the design works (Norman 2013). Figure 2 shows an example of HTA of the following task: *a parent configuring his/her profile full name in a Parental Control interface as shown in the example from* Fig. 1. In Fig. 2, box "0" represents the user's goal that, in this case, is to set his/her full name. The next level, represented by boxes "1", "2" and "3" represents user's mental model with the tasks needed to achieve the respective goal. Finally, the following levels are sub-tasks needed to achieve the goal using the interface considered (see Fig. 1). Comparing different HTAs can show differences on efficiency among different design options.

Smart Toy designers may consider common known usability requirements for design of parental control interface. For example, they can adopt usability principles showed by Alan Dix et al. (2003), usability heuristics of Nielsen and colleagues

---

[5]Hierarchical Task Analysis, by Peter Hornsby at: http://www.uxmatters.com/mt/archives/2010/02/hierarchical-task-analysis.php.

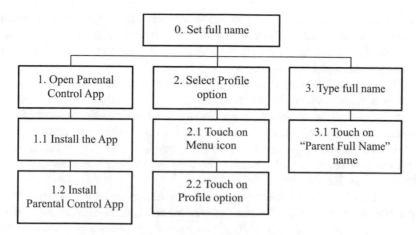

Fig. 2 HTA of an example task using a Parental Control interface

(Nielsen 1994) or Accessibility guidelines as the Web Content Accessibility Guidelines (WCAG 2.0) from the World Wide Web Consortium (W3C)[6]. Other guidelines can also be considered at this point, such as Google Material Design[7] and iOS Human Interface Guidelines[8], according to the devices considered for the Parental Control interfaces. All these kinds of pre-defined requirements can be used for evaluation purposes as well. For this reason, we described it deeply at the *Evaluation* stage section of this chapter.

Finally, in cases when the requirements come from a previous evaluation stage, a restudy of requirements may be done in order to contemplate the new information brought by the outcomes from evaluation methods. After the Requirements stage, the UCD process approaches a (Re)Design stage, which is presented in the following section.

3.2 (Re)Design

Developing applications that fully meet requirements is almost impossible, even for simple applications. Design solutions must consider different perspectives and evolve gradually, cycle after cycle, design and (re)design. Therefore, design should be centered on users, valuing their views and behaviors (Dix et al. 2003; Preece et al. 2015).

---

[6]Web Content Accessibility Guidelines (WCAG) 2.0 website: https://www.w3.org/TR/WCAG20/.

[7]Google Material Design website: https://material.google.com/.

[8]iOS Human Interface Guidelines website: https://developer.apple.com/ios/human-interface-guidelines/.

From users' characteristics and the context where the application will be used, *personas* can be created. *Personas* are a fictional representative description of users' profile. In this sense, *personas* represent not only one, but a whole group of users instead. The use of *personas* can make users' characteristics more clear for development teams, helping them to focus their development in an easier way. The use of personas aims to make the most realistic representation of users during the design process, including specific characteristics and the experience level of users. In addition, they can represent behaviors, attitudes, motivations and goals (Preece et al. 2015). Nevertheless, personas may be time consuming in some contexts related to information security, and methods for quickly creating personas are needed (Bhattarai et al. 2016).

Scenarios of use and sketches of possible solutions can also be done at this stage. Scenarios encompass the most important characteristics of context of use, an important component of usability accessibility, representing them in a rich text format (e.g. including figures of users using the proposed solution) telling stories about typical users interacting with the interface. Sketches and mock-ups can represent early stages of the design, allowing designers to preview it before prototyping the same (Preece et al. 2015).

In sequence, the *Prototype* stage represents the stage for developing design alternatives for the intended product (or its interface) in order to represent different possibilities to accomplish requirements analyzed. After the (Re)Design stage, each design alternative may be prototyped to develop possibilities for evaluations and comparisons with requirements.

3.3 Prototype

The prototype stage corresponds to the period in which creation of prototypes – early representation of specific types – are performed. In UCD cycle, a prototype should be created for each different design alternative conceived by the previous (Re)Design stage. In a next stage, each prototype alternative designed will be evaluated in comparison to users' needs (Preece et al. 2015).

For traditional Web systems, with typical monitor display needed (either desktop or mobile), a wide range of tools is available. These popular tools can be used to prototype many interfaces related to the Smart Toys, as Parental Control. Nonetheless, the following list presents some prototyping tools for traditional Web/mobile applications:

- **Marvel app** – works online or through a mobile app. Available at Marvel app website: marvelapp.com.
- **MockFlow Design Suite** – works online. Available at MockFlow Design Suite website: app.mockflow.com/mockflow/.
- **Cacoo** – works online. Available at Nulab Inc. Cacoo website: cacoo.com.

- **Axure** – requires download. Available at Axure Software Solutions Inc. website: axure.com.
- **Balsamiq** – requires download. Available at Balsamiq Studios website: www.balsamiq.com.

During the initial cycles of UCD process, UCD practitioners may opt for the development of low fidelity prototypes. Low fidelity prototypes are prototypes that implement only the main features planned for the design, or have only representations of the features without a complete implementation, in order to have just the necessary features for evaluation the interface at a sequent stage[9].

Because the development of Smart Toys may be a time-consuming and expensive activity while it involves developing both the toy and additional interfaces (as Parental Control), low fidelity prototypes can be quick to develop and are usually inexpensive. In the context of intelligent systems, such as Smart Toys, the **Wizard-of-Oz (WO)** technique has been generally used, helping developers to present an interactive prototype to final users (Maulsby et al. 1993; Klemmer et al. 2000; Segura and Barbosa 2013). Having an interactive prototype is a desirable situation at the following stage of UCD cycle, because it is required for the conduction of tests with real users.

WO is a rapid prototype technique that simulates the communication of an interface with a user, simulating the way it would behave with all features implemented (Maulsby et al. 1993; Klemmer et al. 2000). WO usually depends on a make-believe situation, which can count on a human operator simulating some feature out of the users' perception (Ashok et al. 2014). Some WO focus on the prototyping of futuristic features, as Smart Toys, while others focus on the understanding of human behavior in specific situations (Maulsby et al. 1993).

In order to better illustrate the procedures for a WO experiment, we have prepared a prototype of a talking doll. The referred Smart Toy was thought to be a User Agent to read Web content for users. At this point, our focus was not on the complete development of a Smart Toy, but on exploring its interactive characteristics in order to provide readers with practical examples. For this reason, we used the following objects to prepare our WO example: a toy (a – Toy) and an Android Device (c – Android Device) connected with a Wireless Sound Box with microphone (b – Wireless Sound Box). Figure 3 shows the components we used to organize our WO example. In this case, we used a handmade doll as the toy.

In sequence, we organized the experiment in order to hide all unnecessary devices from the users' perception. At this moment, we hid the Wireless Sound Box under the toy and asked a one of the authors to keep the Android Device with her in a separate room ("hidden" from users view). During the users' interaction with the prototype, the Team Member could listen and talk to users using the Android device connected with the wireless sound box (that also had a microphone) while reading the Web content at her computer.

---

[9]Usability.gov "Prototyping": https://www.usability.gov/how-to-and-tools/methods/prototyping.html.

Fig. 3 Components for an
example of WO Smart Toy
prototype: a toy (**a** – Toy) and
a Wireless Sound Box (**b** –
Wireless Sound Box)
connected with an Android
Device (**c** – Android Device)

Finally, we used the screens of Fig. 1 in Marvel app in order to make them
interactive, allowing changing screens according to users' touches. Marvel app
allowed us to defined specific areas at each screen that were touchable, and the
respective consequence of touching that area (as changing for another screen).
At this point, we were able to test the whole set of features of the talking doll,
including the Parental Control solution. Another smartphone was used to test the
parental control interface, as shown in Fig. 4. The following section explains in
detail the evaluation methods and techniques that can be used.

3.4 Evaluation

Different evaluation methods have been proposed in the literature. As the UCD
process aims towards the development of usable and accessible interfaces, many of
these methods were proposed aiming to evaluate usability and accessibility. UX may
also be evaluated at this stage, however, it is a recent term and we decided to focus
on well-established methods. For this reason, we decided to approach evaluations
of usability and accessibility, which may also be a way to evaluate some aspects
related with UX – considering the definition of UX showed previously.

Evaluation methods are essential and should not occur only once during
the development process, instead, it must be a periodic activity during the cycles
of the UCD process in order to enhance the level of usability/accessibility of an

Fig. 4 Using Marvel app to test Parental Control interface interactively

interface (Dix et al. 2003; Hornbæk and Stage 2006; Hornbæk 2010; Fernandez et al. 2011; Preece et al. 2015).

Many different methods have been proposed in the literature. For this reason, it is common to find classification for these methods. In this context, the ISO/IEC 25066 (2016) showed evaluation methods divided between: *user-based evaluation* and *inspection-based evaluation*.

3.4.1 User-Based Evaluation

User-based evaluation methods involve participation of a representative sample of end users performing pre-defined tasks with the interface under evaluation. In addition, the exact number of users needed to achieve satisfactory testing outcomes is still being discussed in the literature (Borsci et al. 2013). These testing situations allow the development team to gather important information about usability/accessibility issues that may appear during the test period (ISO/IEC 25066 2016).

A common *user-based evaluation* method is called "usability testing". Although its name, this model of testing can also be applied in order to collect accessibility issues. Usually, usability testing is conducted in a proper laboratory using the Think-Aloud protocol, which aims to help the user to verbalize his/her process of interaction with an interface in order to provide insights of possible usability problems and, consequently, insights for solving them (Ericsson and Simon 1980; Dix et al. 2003; Preece et al. 2015).

The Think-Aloud protocol implies the presence of a test moderator helping and motivating users to verbalize their thoughts related to their interaction process, occurring during test sessions. As users may feel uncomfortable revealing their thoughts, moderators must prepare an ethical consent term informing users about the test purposes, users' roles and rights during testing sessions (including their right of leaving the test sessions whenever they want). It is specially recommended to deeply understand users' characteristics that may imply risks while using the interface. In addition, it is recommended to remind users that they are not being tested during a usability test, but only the interface. Additional material, such as templates, about consent forms can be found at the U.S. Department of Health & Human Services[10].

User-based evaluation methods can also involve video recording and eye-tracking for post analysis (Følstad et al. 2012; Paz and Pow-Sang 2015). These tools help practitioners to gather wider information than only insights from observing users during tests. Video recording allows practitioners to post analyze usability/accessibility characteristics more deeply by analyzing users' behavior carefully. Eye-tracking techniques allow practitioners to verify where users were looking during each stage of the interaction, based on eye-tracking equipment. Examples of video recording and eye-tracker tools that may be used during usability tests are listed as follows:

- **Video-recording**

  - **Morae** – a popular user testing video recording tool among usability practitioners. Morae is a commercial solution and belongs to TechSmith Corporation[11].
  - **UserZoom** – Remote Usability Testing – a software solution for remote usability test on Websites. This software is also a commercial solution and belongs to UserZoom[12].

- **Eye-tracking**

  - **Eye Tribe** – Tracker – the Eye Tribe Tracker is a series of eye-tracker equipment developed by The EyeTribe enterprise. This series of eye-trackers approach traditional peripheral eye-trackers, to be connected to computers,

---

[10]U.S. Department of Health & Human Services Website: www.usability.gov/how-to-and-tools/resources/templates.html.

[11]Retrieved June 13th, 2016, from Morae Website at: www.techsmith.com/morae.html.

[12]Retrieved June 13th, 2016, from UserZoom Website at: www.userzoom.co.uk/software/remote-usability-testing/#content-read=true.

and also a solution for eye-tracking new technologies such as head-mounted displays[13].

- **Tobii** – Tobii eye-tracker series have been developed by Tobii AB enterprise. This group of eye-trackers has traditional eye-trackers to be used with a computer, and new eye-trackers implemented with smart glasses that may allow the eye-tracking of different interfaces users may look at[14].

As Smart Toys are a recent concept in the literature, usability testing practitioners may adapt the characteristic of usability testing of other interfaces for the context of Smart Toys. Some toy computing technologies considered the use of mobile devices together with toys in order to enhance the play experience of players, and also to provide Parental Control solutions (Ng et al. 2015; Rafferty et al. 2015). For these cases, traditional evaluation laboratories equipped with mobile stand support may be appropriated. On the other hand, for evaluating a Smart Toy, which may present anthropomorphic characteristics without a monitor display for users' interactions, solutions such as the eye-tracker glasses may be interesting in order to capture the interaction of users with the whole toy. Future studies can further investigate the applicability of these devices in the evaluation of Smart Toys.

Conducting *user-based evaluations* may be time consuming and involve ethical issues (Hornbæk 2010; Borsci et al. 2013; Munteanu et al. 2015). Additionally, involving end users in evaluations with low fidelity prototypes may imply a barrier for their interaction. For these reasons, usability practitioners may involve different methods during different stages of product development; Methods of usability walkthrough or usability inspection may be used to evaluate usability on design stages when user participation is not adequate for any reason.

3.4.2 Inspection-Based Methods

Evaluation methods considered as inspection usually approach the judgment of evaluators, also called inspectors. In this context, inspectors can be usability specialists, users and different kind of professionals. In these cases, evaluators inspect an interface respecting determined criteria. Additionally, the criteria considered for the evaluation may differ from guidelines, standards, documented principles or good practices (ISO/IEC 25066 2016). The ISO/IEC 25066 (2016) also showed a list of main examples of *inspection-based evaluations* methods that include, but is not limited to: Cognitive Walkthrough, Guidelines Review and Heuristic Evaluation. These examples are described below.

Usability Walkthrough Usability walkthrough methods have a distinct characteristic: can involve usability specialists, end users or other professionals. These participants are called evaluators. In this context, a walkthrough method involves an

---

[13] Retrieved June 13th, 2016, from The EyeTribe Website at: theeyetribe.com/.

[14] Retrieved June 13th, 2016, from Tobii AB Website at: www.tobii.com/group/.

evaluator, or a group of evaluators, playing the roles of users in interaction with a specific interface in order to identify usability problems related to achieve the goal of pre-defined tasks (ISO/IEC TR 25060 2010).

Cognitive walkthrough (CW) is one of the most popular methods among usability walkthrough methods. Lewis et al. (1990) created the first version of the CW method. In sequence, it was revised by Polson et al. (1992) and later by a sequence of studies, as shown by (Mahatody et al. 2010). A CW can be divided into two sequent phases: preparation and evaluation.

At the preparation phase, organizers must choose the tasks that will be base for the CW evaluation. In sequence, the organizers must divide each chosen task into specific actions that compose the respective task; evaluators will follow these actions to continue the evaluation. The preparation phase is also the phase for organizers to describe user profiles and scenario of use for the evaluators.

The second phase of a CW is called the evaluation phase. In the evaluation period, an evaluator must play the role of a user conducting the set of pre-defined actions defined in the preparation phase (Jadhav et al. 2013). The evaluator(s) must conduct each of the pre-defined actions answering four questions related to users' behavior, as follows (retrieved from Mahatody et al. (2010)):

- **Question 1** – *"Will the user try to achieve the right effect?"* – Referring to what users may be thinking when the action begins.
- **Question 2** – *"Will the user notice that the correct action is available?"* – Referring to whether users would be able to locale the command.
- **Question 3** – *"Will the user associate the correct action with the effect that user is trying to achieve?"* – Referring to whether users would be able identify the specific command.
- **Question 4** – *"If the correct action is performed, will the user see that progress is being made toward solution of the task?"* – Referring to user's ability to understand the given feedback.

One can see that all of the questions of a CW are generic enough to be used among different interfaces, such as Parental Control and even Smart Toys themselves. Another advantage of CW method is the easiness of learning to apply it. For this reason, users of different characteristics, such as the elderly, may conduct it. However, the CW evaluation approaches only one component of usability, the "ease of learning" (Wharton et al. 1994).

Many variants of the traditional CW method were proposed in the literature (Mahatody et al. 2010), however, it was out of the scope of the present chapter to describe all of them. Instead, we focused on describing the traditional and widely applied CW method.

Guidelines Review In Guidelines Review, inspectors are called to review the interface in order to find disagreements with a predefined set of usability (or accessibility) guidelines. In this case, the guidelines tend to be specific and numerous, while other principles (as heuristics) are broad (Paz and Pow-Sang 2016). Practitioners can opt among different sets of guidelines according to their needs. Regarding to specific contexts, the literature presented some important sets of guidelines, as the guidelines showed by the World Wide Web Consortium Web Accessibility Initiative (W3C WAI) and the Google Material Guidelines.

Web Content Accessibility Guidelines (WCAG 2.0)   The WCAG 2.0[15] is important for Web interfaces. In our context, it is important in cases when Parental Control is also available online to be accessed via browser. This set is divided among four main principles: Perceivable, Operable, Understandable and Robust. The Perceivable principle refers to the requirement that any information and user interface components must be implemented in order to be perceived by users in some way; the Operable principle refers to the requirement that any feature of the Web system is available for keyboard access; the Understandable principle refers to making the Web content readable and understandable by users; and the Robust, related to the characteristics of the Web content that make it interpretable by user agents, including assistive technology.

For each of these principles, the WCAG 2.0 shows a set of guidelines considered as essential for implementation of the respective principle in the Web. As for the UAAG 2.0 guidelines, WCAG 2.0 also has its own success criteria with levels A, AA, and AAA (further information about WCAG 2.0 success criteria levels can be found at the WCAG portal[16]).

As mentioned previously, reviewing large sets of guidelines may be time consuming for human inspectors. For this reason, the literature has presented Automatized Tools for Guidelines Checking that implements most of the work of a human inspector during a guideline review method. In this context, we indicate the use of two Automatized Tools for Guidelines Checking that implement the checking of WCAG guidelines and are available online: **Web Accessibility Checker (achecker)**[17] and the **TAW tool**[18].

Google Material Design   Google Material Design[19] is a synthesis of good design principles, aiming to gather technology and science. It is a set of guidelines covering *motion*, *style*, *layout*, *components*, *patterns*, *growth & communications* and *usability*. All these guidelines can be used as parameters for evaluation. The main advantage of using Material Design guidelines is to develop interfaces that will follow patterns used by numerous Web and mobile application, especially for Android. In this context, Material Design guidelines can be used for the development of different technologies, varying from websites to smart watch applications.

---

[15] https://www.w3.org/TR/WCAG20/.

[16] WCAG 2.0 success criteria Webpage: www.w3.org/TR/UNDERSTANDING-WCAG20/ conformance.html#uc-levels-head.

[17] Web Accessibility Checker Webpage: achecker.ca/checker/index.php.

[18] TAW tool Webpage: www.tawdis.net/ingles.html?lang=en.

[19] Every information about Google Material Design was retrieved from: https:// material.google.com/#.

For each group of guidelines, Material Design provides an updated platform with descriptions and examples. *Motion* guidelines are used to describe spatial relations and how materials move. In sequence, *style* guidelines provide specifications for colors, icons (with a large set of icons *"available under the Apache License Version 2.0"*[20]), imagery, typography and writing with material design. *Layout* principles are definitions for units and measurements, metrics, structure, responsiveness and principles on how paper is represented with material design. Following, *components* guidelines shows patterns specified for various interface components, as menus, buttons and lists. *Patterns* guidelines present a large set of examples on how to keep your design in consistence with other material applications. The *growth & communications* guidelines aim to help developers to design interfaces that users can easily understand, and intuitively know what they can do with the interface. Finally, *usability* guidelines were divided between *accessibility* and *bidirectionality*.

Accessibility guidelines focus on the development of applications that can be used by people with different abilities. Three main principles structure *accessibility* guidelines: *clear, robust and specific*. *Clear* principle means that users can interact with the app through clear layouts and calls to action. The *robust* principle guide the development of an application that accommodates different users, especially those who need screen-readers, making it easy to access, navigate and understand important tasks. In sequence, the *specific* principle requires that applications must support assistive technologies that are specific for the platform considered.

The second group of *usability* guidelines, *Bidirectionality* guidelines, shows instructions for developing applications that support both left-to-right (LTR) languages and bidirectional languages, such as Arabic.

Google Material Design guidelines are useful for creating good interfaces from the beginning, learning from examples and focusing on wide patterns that have been used by various applications. Evaluation based on Material Design guidelines requires the presence of an inspector reviewing each recommendation from design guidelines and comparing them to the current version of the interface under evaluation, such as a critique method. Material Design guidelines were referred because of their current importance in market, however, as new design guidelines appear, designers may opt for the most appropriated set.

Heuristic Evaluation (HE) Heuristic Evaluation (HE) is one of the most popular methods of *inspection-based evaluation* (Følstad et al. 2012; Martins et al. 2014; Petrie et al. 2015). As CW and Guidelines Review, it involves the presence of inspectors. In HEs, inspectors are responsible to compare interface elements and other usability characteristics against a group of broad usability principles, called heuristics. In this case, heuristics differ from usability guidelines because a unique heuristic may indicate a wide variety of usability problems, depending on each inspector's expertise. This difference from heuristics to guidelines also explain why, usually, heuristic sets has a reduced number of heuristics in comparison to

---

[20]Material Icons Webpage: https://material.io/icons/.

the number of guidelines in a guideline set (Nielsen 1994; Preece et al. 2015; Paz and Pow-Sang 2016).

Jakob Nielsen and his colleagues developed a popular set of usability heuristics, that can be found at the authors website Nielsen Norman Group[21]. The full description for each heuristic can be found at the website, the title of each heuristic is as follows:

1. Visibility of system status.
2. Match between system and the real world.
3. User control and freedom.
4. Consistency and standards.
5. Error prevention.
6. Recognition rather than recall.
7. Flexibility and efficiency of use.
8. Aesthetic and minimalist design.
9. Help users recognize, diagnose, and recover from errors.
10. Help and documentation.

The 10 heuristics of Nielsen and colleagues are popular even for evaluating new contexts such as mobile applications (de Lima Salgado and Freire 2014; de Lima Salgado et al. 2016). For example, Smart Toys are recognized for a unique feature for *"Recognition rather than recall"* (speaking with their users/players), what may be also used for Parental Control interfaces. However, the development of new heuristics for Smart Toys contexts (such as Parental Control interfaces) is recommended and may enhance the potential of the method (Nielsen 1994; Preece et al. 2015).

HE usually evolves the presence of a few evaluators, however, the ideal number of evaluators in a HE is still under discussion in the literature (Nielsen 1992; Borsci et al. 2013). During a HE, evaluators can be helped by organizers in order to fully understand the purpose of the interface.

After the inspection, all evaluators need to gather together in order to discuss a final list of usability problems and propose solutions for such (Nielsen 1994; Preece et al. 2015). Evaluators can rate a severity degree for each problem found, in order to sort a priority order for developers to correct them. Nielsen (1994) showed the following proposal of severity ratings for usability problems:

- **0 – not a usability problem:** it is not a usability problem at all.
- **1 – Cosmetic problem:** it is only a cosmetic problem. Its correction may be made only if extra time is available in the project timeline.
- **2 – Minor problem:** the correction of this kind of problem may receive low priority.
- **3 – Major problem:** the correction of this kind of problem may receive a high priority.

---

[21]10 Usability Heuristics for User Interface Design, by Jakob Nielsen at: https://www.nngroup.com/articles/ten-usability-heuristics/.

- **4 – Usability catastrophe:** these must be the first problems to be corrected. They must be corrected before releasing the product.

HE is an affordable method, easy to learn and fast to conduct but the quality of its outcomes may vary according to the expertise of evaluators (Hertzum and Jacobsen 2001; Preece et al. 2015). Thus, practitioners need to ensure that evaluators have enough experience in the field before conducting a HE.

4   Future Trends: Smart Toys for Elderly and Family Control

Population aging is an interdisciplinary challenge considered an opportunity to innovate and re-design concepts, values, relationships, core societal institutions and products (Cha 2014; Rowe and Kahn 2015). The present generation is probably going to live many years, and it is intuitive to expect that this longer life will be successful and healthy. Nonetheless, it does not mean that the present population will not suffer losses and difficulties; however, these sufferings we may cope, adapt and thrive. The World Health Organization (WHO) considers that future systems need to be realigned from curing diseases to ongoing care of elderly (World Health Organization (WHO) 2015).

Technology has demonstrated potential on decreasing the need of dependents taking care of their elderly, being a substitute or even a complementary for caregiver assistance (Anderson and Wiener 2015). Regarding elderly that live among communities, new technologies have been often mentioned as valuable for communication with family, especially for elderly care (Dishman 2004). On the other hand, for elderly people living alone or institutionalized, the possibility to communicate and share content using digital media can expand the contact network and enhance their close relations, improving family and society (Winstead et al. 2013; Delello and McWhorter 2015). Technologies also made possible carrying out remote monitoring in real time for elderly health. Nevertheless, these technologies were mainly focused on the use by caregivers, so that they send information to the healthcare team (Yuan and Herbert 2011). At this point, developing new technologies that allow family control over situations their elderly live is highly valuable.

The proposal of families monitoring their elderly is important, especially for monitoring accidents related to falls, medical and daily visits of the elderly. However, the concern amongst those involved is that designs of these applications should be simple and easy to use (Warpenius et al. 2015). Yet, despite all these possible applications, many seniors do not use computers, tablets or Smartphones, and have difficulty with tasks in the digital environment.

The elderly may have little motivation to face the challenges of the use of current technology in health care, self-care and remote healthcare services (Bujnowska-Fedak and Pirogowicz 2014). Even when older people have interest on technology for remote healthcare, special attention should be given to those with less education and unfamiliarity with digital devices (de Veer et al. 2015). In this context, studies showed that the elderly would use new technologies for monitoring falls and contact with family (Kurniawan 2008; Cha 2014; Leme et al. 2014; Warpenius et al. 2015).

Regarding difficulties elderly face interacting with traditional interfaces, and their disposition on adopting new technologies in order to enhance their contact with family, we understand that a great opportunity exists for developing Smart Toys for elderly healthcare. Previous studies reinforced that toys have been present in the life of billions of people from all age groups (Hung et al. 2016). In countries such as Canada, it is common to find traditional toys among accommodations of nursing homes. In addition, new technological toys have been used to help elderly with barriers as Alzheimer's disease (CBC News (Canada 2016)). At this sense, future Smart Toys may be evolved by trends in elderly care, and traditional Parental Control interfaces may be evolved to Family Control, allowing chosen relatives to take control of important features of these applications.

4.1 Need for New Methods

Main aspects of UCD may not change because of Smart Toy interfaces, however, specific stages such as evaluation methods may be evolved in order to enhance their applicability and performance in such a context. At this point, regarding inspection-based evaluations, we understand that design guidelines and heuristics may be developed aimed towards the context of Smart Toys. In the context of user-based evaluations, specific technologies (such as eye tracking glasses and versatile cameras) may be needed in order to collect as much data as possible from test sessions. Future studies can explore these topics.

5 Final Remarks

This chapter provided a review of the HCI literature about methods for design of usable and accessible interfaces, with examples focused on Parental Control interfaces in the context of Smart Toys. These methods have been widely applied in HCI literature and can guide the development of diverse applications. Nevertheless, security and privacy are important requirements for Parental Control interfaces. To this extent, security and privacy professionals are still responsible for balancing among usability, security and privacy of such interfaces. Future studies are still needed in order to provided proper methods for balancing usability, security and privacy with less dependency on professionals from such areas.

A few studies have explored development of usability and accessibility methods for Smart Toys or for interfaces related to Smart Toys. Thus, future studies can explore the development of design principles for Usability and Accessibility Inspections, such as guidelines and heuristics, focused on the Smart Toys context. Future studies can also explore the potential of Smart Toys on implementing voice recognition interfaces for Parental Control as a way of enhancing *"Recognition rather than recall"* among Parental Control interfaces, considering possibilities of future Smart Toys working without auxiliary devices for Parental Control interfaces.

Because this chapter presented a review of main UCD methods aiming Parental Control, future studies can extend our scope and explore case studies with real users and their interaction problems with Smart Toys Parental Control.

As future trends, we understand that developing Smart Toys for elderly health-care will be a highly valuable area. In consequence, new approaches will arise with the design of Family Control interfaces. At this point, Family Control may evolve towards the requirements of more users than Parental Control (usually both parents), making it even more challenging for satisfying every user in terms of accepting privacy and security specifications. Additional situations will also need to be discussed, such as what elderly users may control and what will only be under family control.

Acknowledgements This study was supported by the grant #2015/09493-5, São Paulo Research Foundation (FAPESP) .

References

Alshamari M (2016) A review of gaps between usability and security/privacy. Int J Commun Netw Syst Sci 9:413–429. doi:10.4236/ijcns.2016.910034

Anderson WL, Wiener JM (2015) The impact of assistive technologies on formal and informal home care. Gerontol 55:422–433. doi:10.1093/geront/gnt165

Ashok V, Borodin Y, Stoyanchev S et al (2014) Wizard-of-Oz evaluation of speech-driven web browsing interface for people with vision impairments. In: Proceedings of the 11th web for all conference. ACM, New York, pp 12:1–12:9. doi:10.1145/2596695.2596699

Bhattarai R, Joyce G, Dutta S (2016) Information security application design: understanding your users. In: Proceedings of the international conference on human aspects of information security, privacy, and trust. Springer International Publishing, Toronto, pp 103–113. doi:10.1007/978-3-319-39381-0_10

Borsci S, Macredie RD, Barnett J et al (2013) Reviewing and extending the five-user assumption: a grounded procedure for interaction evaluation. ACM Trans Comput-Hum Interact 20:29:1–29:23. doi:10.1145/2506210

Bujnowska-Fedak MM, Pirogowicz I (2014) Support for e-health services among elderly primary care patients. Telemed e-Health 20:696–704. doi:10.1089/tmj.2013.0318

CBC News (Canada) Ludwig the Robot Designed to Help Alzheimer's Patients. https://cacm.acm.org/news/205445-ludwig-the-robot-designed-to-help-alzheimers-patients/fulltext. Accessed 28th Jun 2017

Cha CH (2014) Global population ageing and mission of gerontechnological research and development. Geron 13:65

Chin E, Felt AP, Sekar V, Wagner D (2012) Measuring user confidence in smartphone security and privacy. In: Proceedings of the eighth symposium on usable privacy and security. ACM, New York, pp 1:1–1:16. doi:10.1145/2335356.2335358

de Lima SA, Freire AP (2014) Heuristic evaluation of mobile usability: a mapping study. In: Kurosu M (ed) Human-computer interaction applications and services. Springer International Publishing, Berlin, New York, pp 178–188. doi:10.1007/978-3-319-07227-2_18 de Lima SA, Rodrigues SS, Fortes RPM (2016) Evolving Heuristic Evaluation for multiple contexts and audiences: Perspectives from a Mapping Study. In: Proceedings of the 34th ACM international conference on the design of communication. ACM, New York, pp 19:1–19:8. doi:10.1145/2987592.2987617

de Veer AJE, Peeters JM, Brabers AE et al (2015) Determinants of the intention to use e-health by community dwelling older people. BMC Health Serv Res 15(103). doi:10.1186/s12913-015-0765-8

Delello JA, McWhorter RR (2015) Reducing the digital divide connecting older adults to iPad technology. JAppl Gerontol 36(1):3–28. doi:10.1177/0733464815589985

Dhillon G, Oliveira T, Susarapu S, Caldeira M (2016) Deciding between information security and usability: developing value based objectives. Comput Hum Behav 61:656–666. doi:10.1016/j.chb.2016.03.068

Dishman E (2004) Inventing wellness systems for aging in place. Computer 37:34–41. doi:10.1109/MC.2004.1297237

Dix A, Finlay J, Abowd GD, Beale R (2003) Human computer interaction, 3rd edn. Pearson Education Limited, Harlow, Essex

Ericsson KA, Simon HA (1980) Verbal reports as data. Psychol Rev 87:215–251. doi:10.1037/0033-295X.87.3.215

European Union Safer Internet Program (n.d.) Benchmarking of parental control tools for the onling protection of children. http://sipbench.eu/transfer/SIP_BENCHII_5th_cycle_Executive_summary.pdf

Fernandez A, Insfran E, Abrahão S (2011) Usability evaluation methods for the web: a systematic mapping study. Inf Softw Technol 53:789–817. doi:10.1016/j.infsof.2011.02.007

Følstad A, Law E, Hornbæk K (2012) Analysis in practical usability evaluation: a survey study. In: Proceedings of the SIGCHI conference on human factors in computing systems. ACM, New York, pp 2127–2136. doi:10.1145/2207676.2208365

Gould JD, Lewis C (1985) Designing for usability: key principles and what designers think. Commun ACM 28:300–311. doi:10.1145/3166.3170

Hartson R, Pyla PS (2012) The UX book: process and guidelines for ensuring a quality user experience. Elsevier, Waltham

Hertzum M, Jacobsen NE (2001) The evaluator effect: a chilling fact about usability evaluation methods. Int J Hum Comput Interact 14:421–443. doi:10.1207/S15327590IJHC1304_05

Hornbæk K (2010) Dogmas in the assessment of usability evaluation methods. Behav Inform Technol 29:97–111. doi:10.1080/01449290801939400

Hornbæk K, Stage J (2006) The interplay between usability evaluation and user interaction design. Int J Hum-Comput Interact 21:117–123. doi:10.1207/s15327590ijhc2102_1

Hung PCK, Iqbal F, Huang S-C et al (2016) A glance of child's play privacy in smart toys. In: Sun X, Liu A, Chao H-C, Bertino E (eds) Cloud computing and security. Springer International Publishing, Cham, pp 217–231. doi:10.1007/978-3-319-48674-1_20

ISO 9241-161 (2016) Ergonomics of human-system interaction — Part 161: Guidance on visual user-interface elements. https://www.iso.org/obp/ui/#iso:std:iso-iec:25066:ed-1:v1:en. Accessed 28th Jun 2017

ISO 9241-210 (2010) Ergonomics of human-system interaction — Part 210: Human-centred design for interactive systems. https://www.iso.org/obp/ui/#iso:std:iso:9241:-210:ed-1:v1:en. Accessed 28th Jun 2017

ISO/IEC 25066 (2016) Systems and software engineering — Systems and software Quality Requirements and Evaluation (SQuaRE) — Common Industry Format (CIF) for Usability — Evaluation Report. https://www.iso.org/obp/ui/#iso:std:iso-iec:25066:ed-1:v1:en. Accessed 28th Jun 2017

ISO/IEC TR 25060 (2010) Systems and software engineering — Systems and software product Quality Requirements and Evaluation (SQuaRE) — Common Industry Format (CIF) for usability: General framework for usability-related information. https://www.iso.org/obp/ui/#iso:std:iso-iec:tr:25060:ed-1:v1:en. Accessed 28th Jun 2017

Jadhav D, Bhutkar G, Mehta V (2013) Usability evaluation of messenger applications for Android phones using cognitive walkthrough. In: Proceedings of the 11th Asia Pacific conference on computer human interaction. ACM, New York, pp 9–18. doi:10.1145/2525194.2525202

Katzeff C, Nyblom Å, Tunheden S, Torstensson C (2012) User-centred design and evaluation of EnergyCoach – an interactive energy service for households. Behav Inform Technol 31:305–324. doi:10.1080/0144929X.2011.618778

Klemmer SR, Sinha AK, Chen J et al (2000) Suede: a wizard of Oz prototyping tool for speech user interfaces. In: Proceedings of the 13th annual ACM symposium on user interface software and technology. ACM, New York, pp 1–10. doi:10.1145/354401.354406

Kurniawan S (2008) Older people and mobile phones: a multi-method investigation. Int J Hum-Comput Stud 66:889–901. doi:10.1016/j.ijhcs.2008.03.002

Law EL-C, Roto V, Hassenzahl M et al (2009) Understanding, scoping and defining user experience. Proceedings of the 27th international conference on Human factors in computing systems – CHI 09 719. doi:10.1145/1518701.1518813

Leme RR, Zaina LA, Casadei V (2014) Interaction with mobile devices by elderly people: The Brazilian Scenario. ACHI

Lewis C, Polson PG, Wharton C, Rieman J (1990) Testing a walkthrough methodology for theory-based design of walk-up-and-use interfaces. In: Proceedings of the SIGCHI conference on human factors in computing systems. ACM, New York, pp 235–242. doi:10.1145/97243.97279

Liu B, Lin J, Sadeh N (2014) Reconciling mobile app privacy and usability on smartphones: could user privacy profiles help? In: Proceedings of the 23rd international conference on World Wide Web. ACM, New York, pp 201–212. doi:10.1145/2566486.2568035

Liu B, Andersen MS, Schaub F et al (2016) Follow my recommendations: a personalized assistant for mobile app permissions. In: Twelfth symposium on usable privacy and security (SOUPS 2016)

Mahatody T, Sagar M, Kolski C (2010) State of the art on the cognitive walk-through method, its variants and evolutions. Int J Hum Comput Interact 26:741–785. doi:10.1080/10447311003781409

Martins AI, Queirós A, Silva AG, Rocha NP (2014) Usability evaluation methods: a systematic review. In: Saeed S, Bajwa IS, Mahmood Z (eds). Human Factors in Software Development and Design. IGI Global. Hershey. doi:10.4018/978-1-4666-6485-2.ch013

Maulsby D, Greenberg S, Mander R (1993) Prototyping an intelligent agent through wizard of Oz. In: Proceedings of the INTERACT '93 and CHI '93 conference on human factors in computing systems. ACM, New York, pp 277–284. doi:10.1145/169059.169215

Munteanu C, Molyneaux H, Moncur W et al (2015) Situational ethics: re-thinking approaches to formal ethics requirements for human-computer interaction. In: Proceedings of the 33rd annual ACM conference on human factors in computing systems. ACM, New York, pp 105–114. doi:10.1145/2702123.2702481

Ng G, Chow M, Salgado A d L (2015) Toys and mobile applications: current trends and related privacy issues. In: PCK H (ed) Mobile services for toy computing. Springer International Publishing, pp 51–76

Nielsen J (1992) Finding usability problems through heuristic evaluation. In: Proceedings of the SIGCHI conference on Human factors in computing systems. ACM/Springer, Cham/Heidelberg/New York/Dordrecht/London, pp 373–380. doi:10.1145/142750.142834

Nielsen J (1994) Heuristic evaluation. In: Mack RL, Nielsen J (eds) Usability inspection methods. Wiley, New York, pp 25–62. ISBN 0-471-01877-5

Norman DA (2013) The design of everyday things: revised and expanded edition. Basic books, New York

Paz F, Pow-Sang JA (2015) Usability evaluation methods for software development: a systematic mapping review. In: 2015 8th international conference on Advanced Software Engineering Its Applications (ASEA). pp 1–4. doi:10.1109/ASEA.2015.8

Paz F, Pow-Sang JA (2016) A systematic mapping review of usability evaluation methods for software development process. Int J Softw Eng Appl 10:165–178

Petrie H, Savva A, Power C (2015) Towards a unified definition of web accessibility. In: Proceedings of the 12th web for all conference. ACM, Florence, Italy, pp 1–13. doi:10.1145/2745555.2746653

Polson PG, Lewis C, Rieman J, Wharton C (1992) Cognitive walkthroughs: a method for theory-based evaluation of user interfaces. Int J Man-Machine Stud 36:741–773. doi:10.1016/0020-7373(92)90039-N

Preece J, Sharp H, Rogers Y (2015) Interaction design: beyond human-computer interaction, 4th edn. Wiley, Chichester, West Sussex

Rafferty L, Fantinato M, Hung PCK (2015) Privacy requirements in toy computing. In: PCK H (ed) Mobile services for toy computing. Springer International Publishing, Cham/Heidelberg/New York/Dordrecht/London, pp 141–173

Rowe JW, Kahn RL (2015) Successful aging 2.0: conceptual expansions for the 21st century. J Gerontol B Psychol Sci Soc Sci 70:593–596. doi:10.1093/geronb/gbv025

Segura VCVB, Barbosa SDJ (2013) UISKEI++: multi-device wizard of Oz prototyping. In: Proceedings of the 5th ACM SIGCHI symposium on engineering interactive computing systems. ACM, New York, pp 171–174. doi:10.1145/2494603.2480337

Tang JKT, Tewell J (2015) Emerging human-toy interaction techniques with augmented and mixed reality. In: PCK H (ed) Mobile services for toy computing. Springer International Publishing, Cham/Heidelberg/New York/Dordrecht/London, pp 77–105

Warpenius E, Alasaarela E, Sorvoja H, Kinnunen M (2015) A mobile user-interface for elderly care from the perspective of relatives 40(2):113–124. doi:10.3109/17538157.2013.879148

Wharton C, Rieman J, Lewis C, Polson P (1994) In: Nielsen J, Mack RL (eds) Usability inspection methods. Wiley, New York, pp 105–140. ISBN 0-471-01877-5

Winstead V, Anderson WA, Yost EA et al (2013) You can teach an old dog new tricks: a qualitative analysis of how residents of senior living communities may use the web to overcome spatial and social barriers. J Appl Gerontol 32:540–560. doi:10.1177/0733464811431824

World Health Organization (WHO) (2015) Number of people over 60 years set to double by 2050; major societal changes required. In: .WHO. http://www.who.int/entity/mediacentre/news/releases/2015/older-persons-day/en/. Accessed Nov 17th 2016

Yuan B, Herbert J (2011) Web-based real-time remote monitoring for pervasive healthcare. In: 2011 IEEE International Conference on Pervasive Computing and Communications Workshops (PERCOM Workshops). pp 625–629. doi:10.1109/PERCOMW.2011.5766964

A Security Threat Analysis of Smart Home Network with Vulnerable Dynamic Agents

Laura Rafferty, Farkhund Iqbal, and Patrick C. K. Hung

1 Introduction

The Internet of Things (IoT) describes a network of devices in the physical world, endowed with embedded sensors and networking capabilities. IoT is defined by the International Telecommunication Union (ITU) as "a global infrastructure for the information society, enabling advanced services by interconnecting (physical and virtual) things based on existing and evolving interoperable information and communication technologies" (International Telecommunication Union 2012). The features of IoT that differ from traditional computing include the use of a multitude of devices with embedded sensors and connection to networks, introducing many benefits in terms of automation and optimization. IoT technologies are being widely adopted for a variety of applications including smart grid, industrial control systems, transportation and smart homes. IoT is one of the fastest growing sectors in the technology industry, and applications in the "industrial Internet" have even been compared by General Electric (GE) to the Industrial Revolution due to its projected advancements to productivity and impact on the global economy (Evans and Annunziata 2012). Gartner projected 6.4 billion connected "things" to be in use by the end of 2016 (Gartner 2015). Moreover, this value is projected to increase to 40.9 billion in 2020 (ABI Research 2014) with nearly US$ 9 trillion in annual sales

L. Rafferty (✉) • P.C.K. Hung
Faculty of Business and IT, University of Ontario Institute of Technology, Oshawa, ON, Canada
e-mail: laura.rafferty@uoit.ca;; patrick.hung@uoit.ca

F. Iqbal
Faculty of Business and IT, University of Ontario Institute of Technology, Oshawa, ON, Canada

College of Technological Innovation, Zayed University, Dubai, UAE
e-mail: farkhund.iqbal@zu.ac.ae

© Springer International Publishing AG 2017
J.K.T. Tang, P.C.K. Hung (eds.), *Computing in Smart Toys*, International Series on Computer Entertainment and Media Technology,
DOI 10.1007/978-3-319-62072-5_8

(Nedeltchev 2015). As the number of connected IoT devices is projected to continue to expand over the next years, Forbes identifies 2017 as the year that "the Internet of Everything truly begins" (Newlands 2016).

With IoT expanding to so many industries, one application is the home. With various terms such as connected home, smart home and home automation, Juniper Research defines a smart home as "one that is designed to deliver or distribute a number of digital services within and outside the home, through a range of networked devices" (Sorrell 2015). Smart homes introduce an environment where IoT exists in the context of everyday objects in home, such as fridges, furnaces, televisions and toasters, allowing for greater automation and optimization of daily activities. This can also be extended to smart toys. A smart toy is defined as a device consisting of a physical toy component that connects to one or more toy computing services to facilitate gameplay in the cloud through networking and sensory technologies to enhance the functionality of a traditional toy. A smart toy can be effectively considered an IoT device with artificial intelligence which can provide augmented reality experiences to users. In this context, guests may be unaware of data being collected on them when they are visiting a smart home. When considering smart toys, the main concern is about children who are their main users. Referring to the United States Federal Trade Commission (US FTC) Children's Online Privacy Protection Act (COPPA) and the European Union Data Protection Directive (EUDPD), the definition of a child to be an individual under the age of 13 years old with parental control (Rafferty 2015).

This definition of smart home alludes to information flow outside of home to cloud services, connected vehicles and other external sources in order to provide services to the home, as shown in Fig. 1. The overall goals of smart home technology include making users' lives more comfortable, reducing energy consumption and creating new opportunities. In a smart home environment such as shown in Fig. 2, users can control the lighting, air conditioner, sound system and security systems through a remote interface such as a smart phone or tablet, or from the smart TV. There may be automation, personalized and contextual services provided based on preferences or previous observed behavior, e.g., dimming the lights and turning on the TV when a user sits on the couch at 6 PM. A notification may be sent to the user if a plant needs watering, or even further, a device may automatically water the plant when detected it needs watering. Possibly, an alert can be sent to a healthcare provider if an individual is displaying abnormal behavior symptomatic of a health issue.

Inherently, smart homes require automation and usability features to be built into the design of the system. The sensor and networking capabilities allow the systems to collect and exchange large amounts of data on the user and the environment. With this data, assumptions can be made about user interactions to provide personalized context-aware services and integrate with other technologies such as smart phones and smart watches to further improve user experience. Smart home technologies

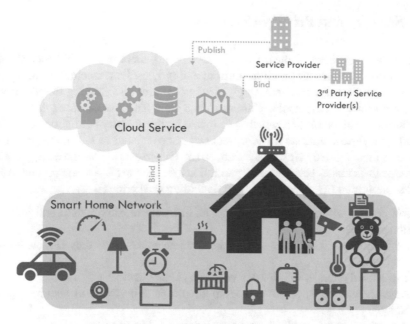

Fig. 1 Smart home services

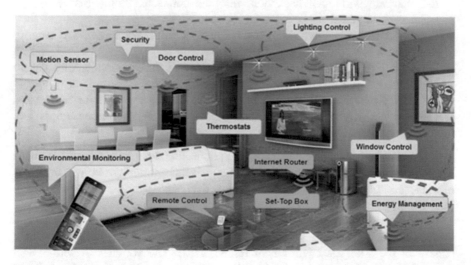

Fig. 2 A sample smart home (Links 2012)

often use a platform or software as a service model, where the mass amounts of data collected are processed and usually stored in the cloud. This architecture differs from the traditional one and creates new opportunities for providing valuable services to users.

2 Security and Privacy Concerns

While the smart home industry is still developing, there are several security and privacy concerns inherent with the current and projected architecture. Industry and research publications are increasingly striving towards encouraging the security of IoT and smart home devices. Current trends show an increase in exploitation of IoT security vulnerabilities, which is followed by the industry predictions for future trends that further indicate a rise in security issues related to IoT, including smart homes (Tagade 2016; Kaspersky Lab 2016; Cybersecurity Ventures, Q4 2016). McAfee Labs makes several threat predictions for the next 2–4 years related to IoT and smart homes (McAfee Labs 2016), including predictions that:

- IoT devices will be useful attack vectors into control, surveillance and information systems.
- Device makers will continue to make amateur mistakes as they IP-enable their products.
- The control plane to IoT devices will be a prime target.
- Aggregation points, where data from devices is collected, will also be a prime target.
- Ransomware will attack internet-enabled medical devices.
- IoT malware will open backdoors into the connected home that could go undetected for years.
- Growth in the number and variety of IoT devices will break some cloud security models.
- Laws will lag behind IoT device technology and its adoption, giving rise to litigation.
- IoT device security will become an important buying criterion for businesses, while privacy will become a more important buying criterion for consumers (i.e., convenience, improved encryption, device anonymity etc.).

The technological advancements in smart home and other IoT technologies have often left security as an afterthought. Users have been beginning to express concerns over the security and privacy of their own data, and manufacturers have been increasingly pressured to respond to such concerns.

Smart home technologies include sensors, monitors, interfaces, appliances and devices networked together to enable automation as well as localized and remote control of the domestic environment (Cook 2012). The volumes of sensor data across a variety of sources, in combination with usage patterns and other inferred information, are growing exponentially and introduce new assets that need to be protected. As more data can be collected from the smart home environment, the home is able to provide more customized services. Sensor data can be collected from a variety of inputs such as microphone, camera, accelerometer and thermometer. Data available to smart home systems can be of volunteered, observed or inferred types: volunteered data is explicitly provided through the user in terms of profile preferences; observed data is collected through sensors such as microphones or usage data; and inferred data refers to information that has been correlated between volunteered and observed data, such as what time a user is likely to return home based on previous usage patterns. Users may be unaware of observed or inferred data that is collected and stored by the system, and this information can possibly become very personal, such as behaviour and life patterns.

Due to the personal value of the data collected and retained by smart home systems, such data can be a target for attackers for a variety of reasons. As sensors are integrated into "things" within the household, collected data can frequently be equated to physical observations, which can be further correlated with information collected from other sensors and sources. As IoT and smart home are typically connected, other devices on the network, including smart phones and wearable devices, are able to interact with each other and share data. This makes it possible for further correlation across devices and for the data to be shared externally. Information collected can become increasingly intimate, such as health information, and can be correlated with data collected from other devices for further context extraction. Therefore, the privacy of all individuals within the home is at risk, including children who may be the primary users of some IoT technologies in the home, such as smart toys. Specifically, this chapter is presented in the context of a smart home network with smart toys (dynamic agents) primarily used by children, presenting unique use cases and concerns for heightened sensitivity of data.

The physical nature of smart homes introduces physical safety risks as well (Shields et al. 2016), since compromised home automation systems might be in control of door locks, health systems or furnaces. Smart home IoT devices may also be mobile or located in sensitive locations, which further raises the severity of security concerns beyond the traditional digital model. Furthermore, the technology limitations implicit with the nature of IoT devices in smart homes introduce new vulnerabilities and attack vectors for potential intrusion into the home network. Although the compromise of a smart lightbulb may not pose immediate risk aside from turning it on or off, if access to the lightbulb allows an attacker to connect and gain control of other devices on the internal network (i.e. lateral movement and escalation of privileges), there are far greater risks.

2.1   Smart Home Security Requirements

As with traditional forms of computing, the security requirements of smart home are confidentiality, integrity, and availability. Balancing these goals with the functionality goals of smart homes, as well as their unique architecture proves to be a challenging task. Smart home systems themselves are dependent on the integrity of data received from sensors. Further, the requirement for availability and convenience to users is of the utmost importance in the smart home, as countering this with stifling security controls would defeat the purpose. For these reasons, a lightweight solution is required for maintaining security of masses of data collected from lightweight endpoints while embracing the functionality goals of the smart home by appearing seamless to the user. While the goal of the smart home is for automation and convenience, users cannot be expected to navigate through hurdles to configure their security controls.

The technology in IoT and smart home introduce new challenges to security differing from traditional computing architectures. These challenges include low processing power and storage available to IoT endpoints leading to lack of adequate endpoint security and encryption. Further, software loaded on devices is often outdated. One study found that software components of home routers were often 4–5 years older than the device (Schneier 2014). Patching or software upgrades are often not possible or are rarely applied. Many IoT devices do not have mechanisms for automated updates. The data is often most vulnerable at sensor/collector level, and when it is in transit at the edge of the network to the cloud. For this reason, endpoints need to be hardened as much as possible, and network communications should be made securely. Internet-facing devices with insufficient authentication, default passwords, or other vulnerabilities such as cross site scripting or code injection create further opportunities for unauthorized external access (Williams and Wichers 2017).

Smart home in particular consist of an array of appliances which can be static or dynamic, each with different security concerns. The large volume of devices creates an increased threat vector. Static devices are often large and are not intended to move around, such as a smart fridge or furnace. Many home appliances have exceedingly long lifespans, such as refrigerators and televisions, which are likely to go without firmware updates, exposing them to threats associated with unpatched vulnerabilities. Dynamic agents such as smart toys are more likely to move around, either independently, or with a user, possibly in and out of the home network. Mobile phones, wearable devices, and smart phones fall into this category. These types of devices are exposed to external threats outside of the home, may connect to unsecured external networks, and expose the devices to external threats. While these devices take the form of traditional home items and appliances, users tend to have higher levels of trust, and are perhaps unaware of the capabilities of these devices if they are abused through security breaches (Canonical 2017). The complex network of devices, likely from multiple vendors and standards, presents further difficulty for achieving a unified approach for security across all devices in the smart home. With the rise in the number of connected devices which may be available in a smart home soon rivaling the number of devices in a mid-sized company, users are faced with the complexity of managing all of these devices without the assistance of sophisticated enterprise security tools or staff to monitor or respond to attacks. Each additional device introduces a new potential threat vector into the home network, which is only as secure as its weakest link.

Often the product development and support structure between third-party manufacturers and suppliers is not conductive to a healthy security posture. Often there is no one entity responsible for the security of IoT devices. Manufacturers may not integrate security into the software development lifecycle, focusing only on functionality. The limited processing and memory resources on the devices also inhibits security solutions to be run on the devices. Third-party manufacturers often do not monitor for vulnerabilities in their old systems or provide updates or support for old models, focusing mainly on the development of future models (L&T Technology Solutions 2014).

Further issues relate to the current smart home environment, which is not yet fully developed and potentially unstable (Higginbotham 2015). Smart home technologies are not always set up correctly by the user, and the technologies are still in beginning stages and do not have enough training data to make fully accurate assumptions of users' preferences, especially for multiple users. There is currently no standard for integrating different device types, while automation requires one universal hub for all devices. There is always a trade-off between security, functionality, and performance. Depending on the situation, there may be different priorities for each of these. In the context of the smart home, there is a high demand for availability and convenience of timely services.

2.1.1   Vulnerabilities and Exploits

Recent publicized security breaches illustrate the severity of the situation and the dire need for effective security solutions across the industry. Countless examples exist including hacked smart fridges, baby monitors (Goodin 2015), WiFi Kettles (Munro 2015, 2016), CCTV Cameras (Tierney 2016), RFID door locks, furnaces, and smart toys such as Hello Barbie (Internet-Connected Hello Barbie Doll Can Be Hacked 2015). There are currently no industry standards governing internet-connected toys, or IoT in general. Smart toys have introduced unique security and privacy concerns in recent years as they have begun to rise in popularity on the market. The physical nature of IoT and smart toys allows for new types of security and privacy threats compared to traditional computing devices. Smart toys are dynamic in nature as they are not restricted to one physical location and can travel with the user. This also increases risk of physical tampering of the device, as well as the risk of connecting to untrusted external networks. Further, while the primary users of toys are children, the presence of a smart toy in the home can trigger the assumption that a child is a resident or guest of the smart home. Child users are sensitive and have unique requirements, while security risks to the smart home can introduce physical safety, security and privacy risks to all members of the household.

The VTech breach in November 2015 characterized the fears of many parents when over 6.3 million children and 4.8 million parents' records were leaked from the company's database (VTech 2016). The customer records associated with VTech toy accounts included childrens' names, genders, birthdates, photos and chat logs, as well as parents' profile information such as addresses, passwords and secret questions. This data was likely accessed by exploiting vulnerabilities to SQL injections in the web interface, while further investigation revealed many other insecure configurations within the (Hunt 2015). This has been the largest known security breach exposing children's records to date, and is the first to illustrate such a widespread. Through password reuse, the data gained from this breach could potentially allow a malicious actor to gain access to a parent's other accounts, including an account used to access the management interface for a smart home.

The security vulnerabilities of childrens' doll, My Friend Cayla, have also been scrutinized by vulnerability researchers such as Ken Munro. While the doll operates through a Bluetooth connection to a smart phone, it does not require authentication for pairing to a device, leaving it open to any device within a 50-foot range which can then access the doll's microphone and voice control. Through the ability to control the voice of the doll, voice commands to control smart home management stations such as Amazon Echo and Google Home can be utilized for malicious intent. This has been exemplified by NCSC's Dr. Ian Levy (Mills 2017), who explained how a My Friend Cayla doll can be used to remotely unlock a voice-controlled smart lock from within the home. While many voice controlled smart locks do not allow remote unlocking for security reasons such as this, it would still be possible for the doll to query for the status of the lock to allow the malicious actor to know if the door had been left unlocked, as well as perform any other set of voice commands accepted by the system.

In regards to other types of smart devices, the authors of (Michele and Karpow 2014) demonstrate a proof-of-concept attack against Samsung Smart TVs, using a malicious media file to exploit vulnerabilities in the media player feature. The researchers were remotely able to gain a permanent backdoor, live A/V stream, perform lateral movement across trusted devices on the network, access and exfiltrate data from across the network. This attack was made possible through vulnerabilities in an open-source library with vulnerabilities published in a public database, easily leveraged by threat actors. Smart TVs are particularly valuable targets as they have powerful hardware and storage capabilities and are located in sensitive environments.

Perhaps the most impactful attacks to IoT devices so far have been related to the Mirai botnet, which as of October 2016, had reached almost every country on earth (Franceschi-Bicchierai 2016). The Mirai botnet has been used to exploit vulnerabilities in a large number of IoT devices to establish a botnet to perform distributed denial of service (DDoS) attacks under its control. While the attack vector was somewhat trivial in targeting internet-facing devices using default credentials, the impact had been devastating. Although the end target of these DDoS attacks is not IoT devices, IoT devices such as DVRs, webcams, and other appliances are being used as a tool for completing illegal activities with excessive impact to targets of the DDoS attacks, such as Internet Service Providers. IoT botnets are one of the biggest threats to Internet stability, and risk is expanding as more devices are created. The implications of these could be devastating as targets could shift to hospitals or critical systems. Prior to the worst of the attacks in October 2016, the FBI had published a public service advisory identifying the risks of IoT devices and opportunities for cybercrime (Federal Bureau of Investigation 2015). This case demonstrates how known vulnerabilities across a mass amount of low-power IoT devices are an easy target for attackers and have high risk of being exploited, even if the device user is not the end target. It also demonstrates a lack of responsibility in the support model for IoT security. In this situation, the owners of the IoT devices are likely unaware that their devices have been compromised. Further, as the device owners are not the main targets, they are virtually unaffected by the attack, aside from some higher than average resource usage. The device suppliers may be blamed for issuing the devices, but the vulnerability is located on a chip by a third party manufacturer.

2.2 Industry Standards and Regulation

A major issue in the IoT industry is the incompatibility of devices. Due to the vast number of devices and many different products and vendors, the industry has been struggling to find a unified approach. This lack of standardization has hindered the development of universal services and full automation as well as created complications for managing the security of the devices. The Alliance for Internet of Things and Innovation (AIOTI) was initiated by the European Commission in 2015. The AOITI Working Group WG03 IoT standardization landscape (Heiles 2015) identifies the organizations acting as major actors in this industry as well as the open source development standards.

The IoT Security Foundation (IoT Security Foundation 2016) is a non-profit organization established to promote security efforts for IoT by providing a mechanism for sharing knowledge, best practices and advice. The IoT Security Foundation's guide entitled "Establishing Principles for Internet of Things Security" outlines several security best practices including designing with security in mind from the beginning, offer appropriate protection for all potential attack surfaces (i.e., device, network, server, cloud, etc.), manage encryption keys securely, verify integrity of software, use a hardware-rooted trust chain, apply authentication and integrity protection to data, identify and revoke compromised or malfunctioning devices, isolate data where applicable, and ensure device metadata is trusted and verifiable. The National Institute of Standards and Technology (NIST) has also published guidelines for managing the security of mobile devices in the enterprise (National Institute of Standards and Technology (NIST) 2013) which can apply to dynamic agents entering the smart home. These guidelines include establishing a mobile device security policy, developing system threat models for mobile devices and the resources accessed through the devices, and reviewing and determining which security services are most relevant to implement. Lastly, according to these guidelines, organizations should regularly maintain mobile device security through methods such as applying upgrades and patches, synchronizing the clock, using access control features, detecting and documenting anomalies, and keeping an inventory of devices.

Government organizations have made statements about recent attacks using IoT infrastructures; however, they have so far not been able to provide an effective legislative solution. In September 2015, the FBI issued a public service announcement stating that "the Internet of Things poses opportunities for cyber crime" (United States Federal Bureau of Investigation 2015), indicating that insufficient security capabilities and complications with patching devices open opportunities for attackers to exploit IoT device weaknesses. Following the Mirai botnet attacks in October 2016, the US Department of Homeland Security in collaboration with NIST released a report on Strategic Principles for Securing the Internet of Things (U.S. Department of Homeland Security 2016). This report identifies the need to prioritize security of IoT devices. This report identifies some key principles for these efforts including:

- Incorporate security at the design phase;
- Advance security updates and vulnerability management;
- Build on proven security practices;
- Prioritize security measures according to potential impact;
- Promote transparency across IoT; and
- Connect carefully and deliberately.

Clearly there many layers of opportunity for security issues for IoT devices in smart homes. While many have argued that security should be provisioned by manufacturers in the development of devices, this is not the current reality. Legislation and regulations attempt to improve security postures, however enforcement of these policies across such a wide target is an extreme task. Although recent advancements are making some improvement, the complexity of this issue spanning across multiple domains does not have an indication of near solution. The smart home network is likely to consist of several endpoints with known vulnerabilities.

3 Security Threat Model

In this section, we investigate the security of smart toys within smart homes from a threat modeling perspective. Threat modeling is a useful tool to assess risk associated with a system and provides a structured approach to security and privacy. Threat modeling can be included as part of the Software Development Lifecycle (SDL). In this section, we aim to identify location privacy threats in a toy computing environment. This section presents a privacy threat model for toy computing with a focus on location privacy.

3.1 Threat Modeling Techniques

Several approaches have been developed for threat modeling, one of the most widely adapted being Microsoft's Threat Modeling Process (Meier et al. 2003) and STRIDE Model (Hernan et al. 2006) for identifying six categories of security threats: Spoofing, Tampering, Repudiation, Information Disclosure, Denial of Service, and Elevation of Privilege. The Open Web Application Security Project (OWASP) has developed their own Application Threat Model (OWASP 2013) which

Fig. 3 Threat modeling process

has some similarities to Microsoft's model. Based on this model, OWASP has also developed a Mobile Threat Model (Open Web Application Security Project (OWASP) 2013) to identify security threats specifically for mobile applications, as well as established a list of the IoT attack surface areas (OWASP 2015). OWASP also recommends Microsoft's STRIDE model for identifying threats.

For a general overview of smart home threat model we have adapted a similar threat modeling approach as Microsoft, as illustrated in Fig. 3. In the following sections we will perform a security threat analysis using this approach. Starting with an overview of the technical architecture, we will identify smart home assets and data flow. Next we will use the STRIDE methodology to identify security threats and threat agents, and review methods of attack through OWASP's IoT attack surface areas. Lastly we will use this analysis to identify security requirements and controls to mitigate threats.

3.2 Architecture Overview

"In the home environment, computer software that plays the role of an intelligent agent perceives the state of the physical environment and residents using sensors, reasons about this state using artificial intelligence techniques, and then takes actions to achieve specified goals" (Crandall et al. 2013). There are several approaches to designing IoT architecture in a smart home environment, as defined by Roman et al. (Roman et al. 2013):

- *Centralized:* A centralized architecture connects the service to the user directly.
- *Collaborative:* The IoT architecture consists of intelligent entities that exchange data.
- *Connected Intranets:* segregated intranets each connect to a central entity, with the possibility of also connecting to each other depending on the configuration.
- *Distributed:* All entities can retrieve, process, combine and provide information or services to other entities.

In a smart home environment, static agents exist as stationary devices within the home (i.e., refrigerator, furnace, heater, etc.). Static agents are likely to never connect to another network or move to a different physical location. They are also less likely to be physically compromised due to the physical security within the home. These are also less likely to be given manual firmware updates and may have unpatched vulnerabilities for long periods of time. Dynamic agents (i.e., mobile

Table 1 Smart home assets

Device	Asset
PC	Files, passwords, browsing history, webcam, microphone
Smart phone	Sensor data, files, passwords, behavior patterns, history, location history, mobility with user
Smart lock	Control of physical access to building
Smart TV	Sensor data (microphone, camera), connectivity to other devices & external network, processing and storage resources
Smart toy	Sensor data (camera, microphone, accelerometer,
Management Station	Connectivity to all smart devices and devices
Router	Connectivity to all devices on network

devices, wearable devices, etc.) are also part of the system and may go in and out of the smart home environment. These devices are more vulnerable to external attacks from physical compromise or connecting to external untrusted WiFi networks. These factors will need to be taken into consideration when considering the trust level of the devices.

While there are several different types of implementations of smart home, for the purpose of this chapter we will focus on one particular architecture type for illustration. The smart home in this scenario contains the following select smart objects as depicted in Table 1: smart TV, smart lock on front door, smart toy (i.e. Hello Barbie). Also present within the home are the following devices: Management station (i.e. Amazon Echo), smart phone, router, and PC. Each of the smart objects are able to connect to the management station to be controlled.

The user is the individual who is within the smart home, interacting with a smart device which is connected to a mobile device also operated by the user. The user interacts with the smart device and/or mobile device through touch screen, microphone, camera, and/or other sensors such as the accelerometer. The physical smart toy may have embedded systems and must be able to interact in some way with the mobile device (ex. physically, visually, audibly, or through a wireless interface). The smart home environment follows the BYOD model, where the mobile device is provided by the user and may take the form of a smartphone or tablet. Behavioural and context data can also be collected and stored on the mobile device, smart device, and/or pushed to the cloud database. Data is stored on the device in flash memory and/or removable storage (i.e. SD card), and communicated over wireless interfaces such as Wi-Fi, Bluetooth, NFC, or RFID. For the purpose of this exercise we can also assume that the smart toy is a dynamic device which is able to move within and outside of the home. Outside of the home network the toy is able to connect to external networks and is physically vulnerable to tampering. Within the smart home environment there are internal and external Human Actors. The human actors have physical or digital access to some or all of the assets within the smart home or cloud. Human actors include: Child (Primary smart toy user), Parents and other smart home occupants (i.e. grandparent, pet, guest, other), and Service provider. There can also be a potential malicious external actor with access to the devices or data.

Microsoft recommends to divide the architecture into zones for: device, field gateway, cloud gateway, and services (Diogenes and Betts 2017). These zones can be used for trust boundaries, where data transitioning between these boundaries can be subject to threats outlined in the following section. The device zone is the space around the device (smart tv, smart lock, etc.) for physical access and/or local network access. Field gateway is a device or appliance, in this case the management station, which acts as a hub for device control, and enables communication and device data processing. The cloud gateway allows remote communication with devices, data processing and services, located in an external cloud environment. Lastly, the services zone is for the services provided to the devices for data collection and analysis, as well as control through a management interface.

3.3   Assets and Data Flow

3.3.1   Identification of Assets

Assets within the smart home include all physical and digital assets associated with the home and its occupants, including but not limited to the below items. It is also important to note that in the case of smart toys where the user is most likely a child under the age of 13, their personal information is particularly sensitive especially when associated with their real identity.

Physical Assets

- Physical safety of occupants (i.e., child, parent, grandparent, pet, other);
- Valuable and sentimental items (jewelry, electronics, furniture, heirlooms, etc.);
- Other household items (dishes, soap, food, clothing, etc.);
- Sensitive physical documents; and
- Appliances controlling physical environment (furnace, door lock, healthcare device).

Digital Assets

- Personally identifiable information (name, address, bank account, etc.);
- Context data (observed, volunteered or inferred data on occupants) including preferences and behavior/movement patterns;
- Intellectual property (developing patent, source code, unpublished research works, etc.);
- Passwords;

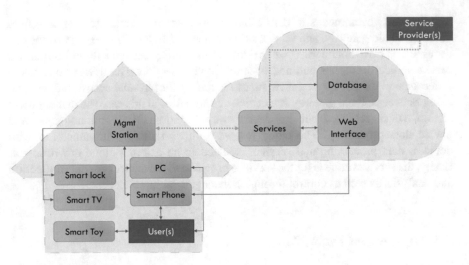

Fig. 4 Smart home data flow diagram

- Access to external networks (i.e., remote access to a user's work computer, email, social networks, etc.); and
- Processing resources on devices.

3.3.2 Data Flow

In the Data Flow Diagram (DFD) illustrated in Fig. 4, the occupants of the smart home are able to interact with the smart devices in the environment through sensors, voice control and other interfaces. For example, to turn on a Smart TV a user can walk into the room and use voice control to turn on the TV. The user also has a device such as a smart phone, which includes an application to control the devices in the smart home. The smart devices may connect to the smart phone through bluetooth, or connect to the management station over Bluetooth or WiFi. Services are provided through an external cloud service managed by a service provider. There is also a web interface located externally within this cloud where the user is able to manage their devices. While the smart home devices exist in a physical environment, the devices also have the potential to interact with eachother in the physical plane, through sensors, microphones, cameras, and other networking capabilities. The other physical objects within the home can be perceived by the sensors although they are not depicted in the diagram. A PC is also likely to be located within the home, which can contain other sensitive files and user data.

3.3.3   Security Threats

Identify Security Threats

Microsoft provides a widely adopted model for grouping of threats into six categories for threat modeling purposes known as the STRIDE Threat Model. These can also be applied in the context of a smart home environment. The security threats outlined in the STRIDE threat model are outlined as follows (Microsoft 2005):

- **Spoofing Identity**: an agent is able to falsely identify itself as another agent.
- **Tampering**: unauthorized modification of data. The mobility of a dynamic agent such as a smart toy leaves it vulnerable to tampering if it is physically available to a malicious agent.
- **Repudiation**: an agent is able to deny performing an action without being able to be proven otherwise.
- **Information Disclosure**: exposure of information to an agent for whom it was not intended. A malicious agent with control of a My Friend Cayla doll can overhear conversations within the household.
- **Denial of Service**: disruption of services. Compromised devices within the home can be used in large-scale Distributed Denial of Service (DDoS) attacks. Alternatively, if a malicious agent is able to gain access into the network, they can perform denial of service attacks to disable devices or services within the home.
- **Elevation of Privilege:** An entity is able to gain privileged access to data or control of resources.

Mapping Privacy Threats to DFD

Referencing the DFD from Fig. 4, we will now outline the DFD elements and then map the privacy threats to the DFD. Table 2 shows the DFD elements in the smart home architecture mentioned in the previous section.

Table 2 Mapping DFD elements to security threats

Entity	User
	Service provider
	Device
	External entities
Process	Device management
	Smart services
Data store	Local endpoint data
	Service database
Data flow	User data stream (user to device)
	Device data stream (device to gateway)
	Service data stream (device to service/cloud)
	Cloud data stream (gateway to cloud)

Table 3 Mapping privacy threats to DFD elements

Threat categories	Entity	Process	Data store	Data flow
Spoofing	x	x		
Tampering		x	x	x
Repudiation	x	x	x	
Information disclosure		x	x	x
Denial of service	x	x	x	x
Elevation of privilege		x		

x = Vulnerable

Based on the above DFD elements, Table 3 maps the STRIDE security threats to DFD element types (Entity, data flow, data store, process) in a smart home scenario with the smart toy example:

Entities (users, service providers, and devices), are vulnerable to potential spoofing, repudiation and denial of service attacks. Processes such as device management and smart services are vulnerable to all of the potential STRIDE threats. Data stores on the endpoints and databases can be vulnerable to tampering, repudiation (in some situations), information disclosure and denial of service. Finally, the data flow between devices, field gateway, cloud gateway and services can be vulnerable to tampering, information disclosure and denial of service. The next section will review possible methods of attack for each of these threats.

3.4   Methods of Attack

In this section we will observe different methods an attacker can use to achieve the threats described in the previous section. OWASP has compiled a list of the IoT attack surface areas (OWASP 2015) which will be analyzed in Table 4 below in the context of a smart home. For the purpose of this chapter, we will focus on the security considerations directly applicable to dynamic agents such as smart toys which are vulnerable to physical tampering and insecure networks. Specific to the device, there is potential for firmware extraction and malicious updates. Weak or default passwords, SQL injection and cross-site scripting vulnerabilities on the device web interface can be easily taken advantage of by malicious actors. Further, on an untrusted network, insecure communications between the smart toy and/or mobile device can be intercepted. Other vulnerabilities which are applicable to smart homes but are not further mentioned include the administrative interface and cloud web interface, and vendor and third-party back-end APIs.

Table 4 OWASP IoT attack surface areas (OWASP 2015)

Attack surface	Threats/vulnerablities
Device physical interfaces	Firmware extraction [T,I] User/admin CLI [I,E] Privilege escalation [E] Reset to insecure state [S,R,I,D,E] Removal of storage media [S,T,R,I,D]
Device web Interface	SQL injection [S,I,E] Cross-site scripting [S,I,E] Cross-site request forgery [S,I,E] Username enumeration [S] Weak passwords [S,R,E] Account lockout [D] Known default credentials [S,R,E]
Device firmware	Hardcoded credentials [E] Sensitive information disclosure [I] Encryption keys [I]
Update mechanism	Update sent without encryption [S,I] Updates not signed[S] Update verification [S] Malicious update[T]
Device memory	Cleartext usernames/passwords [S,I,E] Third-party credentials [S,I,E] Encryption keys[S,I,E]
Local data storage	Unencrypted data [I] Data encrypted with discovered keys [S] Lack of data integrity checks[R]
Device network services	Information disclosure [I] User/admin CLI [I,E] Injection[T] Denial of service [D] Unencrypted services/poorly implemented encryption [I] Test/development services [I] Buffer overflow [T,E] UPnP[I,E] Vulnerable UDP services [I,E] DoS [D]
Mobile application	Implicitly trusted by device or cloud [I,E] Username enumeration [I] Account lockout [D] Known default credentials/weak passwords [S,I,E] Insecure data storage [I] Transport encryption [I] Insecure password recovery mechanism [S,I,D,E]
Ecosystem access control	Implicit trust between components [S,I,E] Enrollment security [S,R,E] Decommissioning system [S,R,I,D] Lost access procedures [S,R,I,D,E]
Network traffic	LAN [S,I,D] LAN to internet [S,I,D] Short range (Bluetooth) [S,I,D]

3.5   Security Requirements/Controls

Based on the above analysis, this section now discusses some security requirements and controls needed to mitigate these threats described in the previous section. The security requirements for IoT and smart homes are combination of web application and mobile security requirements, as well as new considerations for the cloud environment. Dynamic agents introduce new types of vulnerabilities while they are able to move in and out of the home network, becoming susceptible to physical compromise, tampering and network attacks. The below security requirements are required to address the vulnerabilities specific to this architecture.

- Management:
    - Web interface form validation & protection against web attacks (SQL injection and cross-site scripting)
    - Secure enrolment of devices and management
    - Do not implicitly trust devices on network/cloud
- Network:
    - Secure update mechanisms (encryption, signatures, trusted source only)
    - Enforce encryption in transit
- Credentials:
    - Do not store credentials in plaintext
    - Enforce strong password requirements
    - 2-factor authentication requirements from external untrusted networks

Our threat model illustrates that the security requirements for smart home environments with dynamic agents require special attention to the local and network security of the agent. While this can also be applicable to other types of smart home and IoT devices, the risk is much higher with dynamic agents such as smart toys due to their increased exposure.

4   Discussion

While vulnerabilities of IoT devices are provably high, the consequences of many attacks (i.e., turning a light bulb on and off) are often low impact. Intent can be for political, military, economic, or social benefit, which often are not relevant enough to most threat actors to generate enough motive to compromise a smart home device unless it is for a greater purpose. Currently, the profit value for criminals is unclear, however the next few years may unfold some demonstrated value (Lewis 2015). So far, the highest demonstrated risk to IoT compromise has been for the purpose of recruiting members of IoT botnets, in order to pursue larger scale DDoS activity targeting alternate systems, or perpetuating spam campaigns. So far, more complex attacks have been demonstrated only targeting individual systems and have not been effective at a mass scale. However, there is some potential for other types of mass-scale attacks such as spanning multiple smart homes in a neighborhood to simultaneously cut off their power. Ransomware has been a popular trend in 2016, which has potential to move towards IoT and smart home devices.

Alternatively, using a vulnerable IoT device as an attack vector to advance into the home network is another possibility, with a spectrum of consequences. Other motives for attacks that are highly targeted towards a particular user are generally unlikely in the current threat landscape, however it is very possible for this to develop, especially by APT groups. If there are other ways to easily extract credit card or other banking information from users through this vector, it will surely be exploited as well. The consequences of compromised IoT and smart home appliances will continue to increase in severity as IoT makes its way into more critical aspects of life, for example, health care devices. Consequences threatening the physical safety of users, loss of life or significant economic harm are the most critical. While the likelihood of highly targeted attacks is very low, the exposure of highly personal data, as well as potential for full control over a home raises many concerns.

5   Conclusion

This chapter provides a security analysis of a smart home environment with dynamic smart toy agents. We provide an overview of smart home and smart toy security issues, followed by a security threat model to illustrate these threats. While smart home and smart toy technologies continue to evolve and introduce new capabilities, security issues can become more impactful to the safety and wellbeing of their users.

References

ABI Research (2014) The internet of things will drive wireless connected devices to 40.9 billion in 2020. Retrieved Nov 2016, from https://www.abiresearch.com/press/the-internet-of-things-will-drive-wireless-connect/

Canonical (2017) Taking charge of the IoT's security vulnerabilities. Ubuntu, Douglas, https://pages.ubuntu.com/IoT-Security-whitepaper.html

Cook DJ (2012) How smart is your home? Science 335(6076):1579–1581

Crandall AS, Krishnan NC, Thomas BL, Cook DJ (2013) CASAS: a smart home in a box. Computer 46(7):62–69

Cybersecurity Ventures (Q4 2016) Cybersecurity market report: market sizing & projections. Cybersecurity ventures. Retrieved from http://cybersecurityventures.com/cybersecurity-market-report/

Diogenes Y, Betts D (2017) Internet of things security architecture. Retrieved May 2017, from Microsoft Azure: https://docs.microsoft.com/en-us/azure/iot-suite/iot-security-architecture

Evans PC, Annunziata M (2012) Industrial internet: pushing the boundaries of minds and machines. General electric

Federal Bureau of Investigation (2015) Public service announcement: internet of things poses opportunities for cybercrime. United States Federal Bureau of Investigation, Washington, DC. Retrieved from https://www.ic3.gov/media/2015/150910.aspx

Franceschi-Bicchierai L (2016) Internet of things malware has apparently reached almost all countries on earth. Motherboard. Retrieved Apr 2017, from https://motherboard.vice.com/en_us/article/internet-of-things-mirai-malware-reached-almost-all-countries-on-earth

Gartner (2015) Gartner Says 6.4 Billion Connected "Things" Will be in Use in 2016, Up 30 Percent from 2015. Retrieved Nov 2016, from http://www.gartner.com/newsroom/id/3165317

Goodin D (2015) 9 baby monitors wide open to hacks that expose users' most private moments. Retrieved 5 Dec 2016, from http://arstechnica.com/security/2015/09/9-baby-monitors-wide-open-to-hacks-that-expose-users-most-private-moments/

Heiles J (2015) AIOTI WG03 IoT standardisation. Platforms for connected factories of the future workshop. Brussels. Retrieved from http://ec.europa.eu/information_society/newsroom/image/document/2015-44/11_heiles_11948.pdf

Hernan S, Lambert S, Ostwald T, Shostack A (2006) Uncover security design flaws using the STRIDE approach. MSDN Magazine.

Higginbotham S (2015) 5 reasons why the 'smart home' is still stupid. (Fortune) Retrieved 5 Dec 2016, from http://fortune.com/2015/08/19/smart-home-stupid/

Hunt T (2015) When children are breached – inside the massive VTech hack. Retrieved Dec 2015, from Troyhunt.com: https://www.troyhunt.com/when-children-are-breached-inside/

International Telecommunication Union (2012) Series Y: global information infrastructure, internet protocol aspects and next-generation networks – overview of the internet of things. Telecommunication Standardization Sector of ITU (ITU-T).

Internet-Connected Hello Barbie Doll Can Be Hacked (2015) Retrieved 5 Dec 2016, from http://www.pcworld.com/article/3012220/security/internet-connected-hello-barbie-doll-can-be-hacked.html

IoT Security Foundation (2016) About Us. (IoT Security Foundation) Retrieved 5 Dec 2016, from https://iotsecurityfoundation.org/about-us/

Kaspersky Lab (2016) Predictions for 2017: 'indicators of compromise' are dead. Kaspersky Security Bulletin.

L&T Technology Solutions (2014) Security considerations for internet of things. L&T Technology Solutions.

Lewis JA (2015) Managing risk for the internet of things. Center for Strategic and International Studies (CSIS), Washington, DC

Links C (2012) The new smart home is the really smart home. Retrieved Apr 2017, from Wireless Design Magazine: https://www.wirelessdesignmag.com/blog/2012/09/new-smart-home-really-smart-home

McAfee Labs (2016) 2017 threats predictions. Intel Security.

Meier J, Mackman A, Dunner M, Vasireddy S, Escamilla R, Murukan A (2003) Chapter 3: threat modeling. In: Improving web application security: threats and countermeasures. Microsoft Corporation. Retrieved from https://msdn.microsoft.com/en-us/library/ff648644.aspx

Michele B, Karpow A (2014) Watch and be watched: compromising all smart TV generations. IEEE 11th Annual Consumer Communications & Networking Conference (CCNC) – Security Privacy and Content Protection. Las Vegas

Microsoft (2005) The STRIDE threat model. Retrieved Apr 2017, from Microsoft Developer Network: https://msdn.microsoft.com/en-us/library/ee823878(v=cs.20).aspx

Mills K-A (2017) Hackers can unlock your home's front door with innocent looking DOLL and you won't even know they've done it. Retrieved Apr 2017, from Mirror: http://www.mirror.co.uk/news/uk-news/hackers-can-unlock-your-homes-9816119

Munro K (2015) New Wi-Fi kettle, same old security issues? Meh. Retrieved 5 Dec 2016, from https://www.pentestpartners.com/blog/new-wi-fi-kettle-same-old-security-issues-meh/

Munro K (2016) Yet another vulnerability in the smarter Wi-Fi Kettle. Retrieved 5 Dec 2016, from https://www.pentestpartners.com/blog/yet-another-vulnerability-in-the-smarter-wi-fi-kettle/

National Institute of Standards and Technology (NIST) (2013) Guidelines for managing the security of mobile devices in the enterprise. United States Department of Commerce. NIST Special Publication 800–124. Retrieved from http://nvlpubs.nist.gov/nistpubs/SpecialPublications/NIST.SP.800-124r1.pdf

Nedeltchev P (2015) The internet of everything is the new economy. Retrieved Nov 2016, from http://www.cisco.com/c/en/us/solutions/collateral/enterprise/cisco-on-cisco/Cisco_IT_Trends_IoE_Is_the_New_Economy.html

Newlands M (2016) 6 disruptive trends in technology for 2017. Retrieved 6 Dec 2016, from http://www.forbes.com/sites/mnewlands/2016/08/31/6-disruptive-trends-in-technology-for-2017

Open Web Application Security Project (OWASP) (2013) OWASP Mobile Security Project – Mobile Threat Model. Retrieved Feb 2015, from https://www.owasp.org/index.php/Projects/OWASP_Mobile_Security_Project_-_Mobile_Threat_Model

OWASP (2013) Application threat modeling. OWASP. Retrieved from https://www.owasp.org/index.php/Application_Threat_Modeling

OWASP (2015) IoT attack surface areas (draft). Retrieved May 2017, from OWASP IoT Attack Surface Areas Project: https://www.owasp.org/index.php/IoT_Attack_Surface_Areas

Rafferty L (2015) A location privacy model and framework for mobile toy computing. University of Ontario Institute of Technology, Canada

Roman R, Zhou J, Lopez J (2013) On the features and challenges of security and privacy in distributed internet of things. Comput Netw 2013(57):2266–2279

Schneier B (2014) The internet of things is wildly insecure – and often unpatchable. (Schneier on Security) Retrieved 5 Dec 2016, from https://www.schneier.com/essays/archives/2014/01/the_internet_of_thin.html

Shields T, Pelino M, McClean C, Duong J, Maxim M, Blackborow J, Dostie P (2016) Secure IoT as it advances through maturity phases: predict and prevent attacks targeting the internet of things. Forrester. Retrieved from https://www.forrester.com/report/Secure+IoT+As+It+Advances+Through+Maturity+Phases/-/E-RES128642

Sorrell S (2015) Connected homes: getting smarter. Juniper Research, Hampshire

Tagade K (2016) Top 7 cyber-security predictions for 2017 and beyond. (iamwire) Retrieved 6 Dec 2016, from http://www.iamwire.com/2016/12/top-7-cyber-security-predictions-for-2017-and-beyond/145494

Tierney A (2016) Pwning CCTV cameras. Retrieved 5 Dec 2016, from https://www.pentestpartners.com/blog/pwning-cctv-cameras/

U.S. Department of Homeland Security (2016) Strategic principles for securing the Internet of Things (IoT). U.S. Department of Homeland Security. Retrieved Nov 2016, from https://www.dhs.gov/sites/default/files/publications/Strategic_Principles_for_Securing_the_Internet_of_Things-2016-1115-FINAL_v2-dg11.pdf

United States Federal Bureau of Investigation (2015) Public service announcement: internet of things poses opportunities for cyber crime. Retrieved Nov 2016, from https://www.ic3.gov/media/2015/150910.aspx

VTech (2016) FAQ about Cyber Attack on VTech Learning Lodge. Retrieved Apr 2017, from VTech Press Releases: https://www.vtech.com/en/press_release/2016/faq-about-cyber-attack-on-vtech-learning-lodge/

Williams J, Wichers D (2017) OWASP Top 10: the ten most critical web application security risks. The Open Web Application Security Project (OWASP)

Privacy Preservation Framework for Smart Connected Toys

Benjamin Yankson, Farkhund Iqbal, and Patrick C. K. Hung

1   Introduction

Although the origin of the word "toy" is unknown, it is believed that it was first used in the fourteenth century (Shop 2016). However, toys have been in existence since time immemorial. Toys have been part of every culture as a uniquely design product for learning, socialization, leisure, play, and intended to benefit children as they go through various developmental stages. The progression of primitive toys included rocks and pinecones, to modern dolls, stuffed animals and trains (Rafferty L 2015). As new ideas continue to develop to reflect the era and culture, it proved that the toy is a product which has evolved along the changes. Toy companies have embraced modern technologies such as mobile technology into the design of their products; reshaping the concept of toys and education through mobile applications and augmented reality (LaMonica 2015). Toy computing has unique requirements, including specific needs for children, as well as the relationship between the child, mobile device, and physical toy component. These toys are intended to provide children opportunities to learn, interact, and play. Each cultural or generation have

B. Yankson (✉)
Faculty of Business and IT, University of Ontario Institute of Technology, Oshawa, ON, Canada

Faculty of Applied Computing, Sheridan College Oakville, Ontario, Canada
e-mail: benjamin.yankson@sheridancollege.ca

F. Iqbal
Faculty of Business and IT, University of Ontario Institute of Technology, Oshawa, ON, Canada

College of Technological Innovation, Zayed University, Dubai, UAE
e-mail: farkhund.iqbal@zu.ac.ae

P.C.K. Hung
Faculty of Business and IT, University of Ontario Institute of Technology, Oshawa, ON, Canada
e-mail: patrick.hung@uoit.ca

© Springer International Publishing AG 2017

J.K.T. Tang, P.C.K. Hung (eds.), *Computing in Smart Toys*, International Series on Computer Entertainment and Media Technology,
DOI 10.1007/978-3-319-62072-5_9

Fig. 1 Basic toy made of
wood (Courtesy of National
Museum of Australia: http://
www.nma.gov.au/collections/
highlights/toy-tractor)

Fig. 2 Sophisticated toy
design (Courtesy of
VirtualWolf https://www.
flickr.com/photos/virtualwolf/
4976758560)

built on the functionality of toys and intended purpose of play. The toy design
have changed from basic carving of wood (Fig. 1) or stone forms to sophisticated
design with outward appearance of modeled after a teddy bear (Fig. 2). The latter
form not only provides a sense of cuteness, trusting and comforting feel for children,
but also have a full interactive functionality and the capacity to process language and
guidance, as well as to engage in deeper communication with its environment and
the children. Other than the parents of the child, most children initiate interactions
between other children and the toys given by their caretakers. Younger children use
toys to discover their identity, train their bodies become stronger, learn causes and
effects, explore relationships, and practice skills that they may need when grown up
(Anikweze 2014).

There have been many new toys that were "scary" when they were introduced,
including video game consoles, dolls that are capable to move, interactive toys like
the Furby, and the attention hungry Tamagotchi digital pets (Smith 2016). As our
lives have become ever more "connected", it's not surprising that manufacturers
have begun to create toys that are connecting to the Internet in order to enhance their
interaction with children (Smith 2016). These kind of new product or sophisticated
design model is called a smart connected toy (SCT), which includes tangible
objects with electronic components can facilitate bilateral interactions between
children and itself to carry out a purposeful task (Kara 2013). It general built
to talk, learns, remembers and can respond to a child request. Basic feature
sets include but not limited to voice recognition, image recognition, jokes and
storytelling, are personable. On the fundamental level, it works through some form

of connectivity (either Bluetooth or Wi-Fi), and can download software and conduct activity through WiFi to a connected source in the cloud. It can also have a basic scanning technology, a microphone used to capture voice for further processing through an interface. Some Smart toys are built as part of Internet of Things (IoT) with capability of providing: Location based services (LBS), Mobile advertisement (MA), Geo-social network applications (GeoSNs), and contextual data collection (Rafferty L 2015).

Most smart toys in the market has restrictions on type of question they answer, and usually will not answer question regarding mature content. For example, ToyTalks' Hello Barbie smart toy has limited canned responses, whiles Cogni-Toy's Dino uses IBM Watson to respond to arbitrary questions with limitation (Mcreynolds and Hubbard 2017). With this limitation on question children can ask, current toys in the market also does not provide any feedback mechanism to parent of the child behavior or mature content inquiry. Although such lack of feedback on activities between the toy and the child should be discouraging and concerning, ongoing research works within toy computing arena demonstrate that anthropomorphic design results in greater engagement and trust for users (Rafferty LB 2015); allowing children to build strong bond with these toys. The anthropomorphic design leads to children unconsciously engaging with these devices as their trusted confident. Therefore, divulging significant personal and family information to the toy which then is synch to extended resource like the cloud. Some of the information divulged, if compromised, can inadvertently put the child safety at risk. As per recent study, the authors found that children are often unaware that the toys record what is said to them (Mcreynolds and Hubbard 2017).

Because of SCT connectivity, it faces the same risk and vulnerability as any connected device. Unlike the other connected devices, these toys are always on, blending into the background until needed (Mcreynolds and Hubbard 2017). As a result, there is serious concern for security and privacy of user's data. Cybercriminals are looking to exploit connected toys as with any device connected to the internet. For example, according to ESET (Welive Security), an IT security company that offers anti-virus and firewall products, the 5 most devastation attacks in 2015 includes a hack into a toy manufacture Vtech (WeLiveSecurity 2016). Vtech a consumer electronics manufacturer, which specializes in educational toys and technology for children, was hit by a data breach in November 2015 affecting approximately 6.4 million children and 4.9 million customer (parent) accounts worldwide (WeLiveSecurity 2016). The compromised data included child profiles (names, genders and birthdays), passwords, IP addresses, download history, gender and birth dates. Although the culprit was arrested the data still exist out on the internet and can potential be used for malicious activity against these families. Such incident which can lead to data breach is not just limited to Vtech issue. Other known vulnerabilities which can be exploited includes but not limited to Fisher-Price Smart Toy – R7-2015-27 improper authentication handling (CVE-2015-8269), hereO GPS platform–R7-2015-24 authorization bypass, and Hello Barbie Poodle attack (WeLiveSecurity 2016).

Children privacy should be a major concern for parents who wish to protect their children from potential harm, which inadvertently can result from play information or context information shared by the toy. In a worst case scenario, context information, such as location, can allow a child predator intending to harm your child to identify his/her location and therefore trace back to your child. This scenario can be any parent worse nightmare. Many countries have safety standards and regulations limiting the types of ordinary non-connected toys that can be sold within it market. Generally, these measures are in place to protect the safety of the public, especially children (Rafferty LB 2015). For example, in Canada, according to Industry Guide to Health Canada's Safety Requirements for Children's Toys and Related Products, toys containing lead cannot be sold in stores (HealthCanada 2017). Other proposed restriction to keep children safe includes but not limited to mechanical hazards, flammability hazards, microbiology hazards, etc. Similar standards or requirement exist in Europe and the USA; which sole goal is to protect children safety. While there have been many efforts by governments and international organizations, such as the United Nations Children's Fund (UNICEF) and Children's On-line Privacy Protection Act (COPPA) in the United States, to encourage the protection of children data online, there is currently no standard privacy protection framework for smart toys (Hung 2015). In Canada, children are protected by international regulations such as the United Nations Convention on the Rights of the Child (CRC), which protects children from all forms of violence, exploitation and abuse and discrimination, and ensures that the child best interest should be the primary consideration in any matters affecting them (Rafferty LB 2015). Canadas' Information privacy laws such as the Personal Information Protection and Electronic Documents Act (PIPEDA) have been developed to protect the online privacy of users, including children (Rafferty LB 2015). It is of great concern to Canadian parents that the toys and mobile services which their children have access to comply with these privacy laws, for the safety and protection of their children. To our understanding, toy safety guidelines are out of date and out of synch with the current innovations in smart toy technology. Toy safety guidelines such as Health Canada's safety requirements for Children's toys and Related Products concentrate on physical safety related to traditional toys and do not mention any restrictions related to smart toys and mobile services. Considering its current context where safety issues are still a challenge for government, society and the public (Rafferty LB 2015). Besides concerns about companies collecting data, these toys also raise potential ethical concerns such as parents spying on their children (Mcreynolds and Hubbard 2017).

The motivation behind this chapter includes but not limited to helping address child safety and privacy concerns with context data(location, and historical data); which be used to predict child movement, privacy absence, and co-location data. In dealing with context data of SCT, the idea is to consider ways of protection of child innocence, safety and privacy while building trusted smart toys without stifling innovation. In Canada for example, no specific privacy regulation addressing this vulnerable sector exist, so proposing common best practice as part of Smart Connected Toy Privacy Common Body of Knowledge (CBK) for child safety, is critically needed for protecting children.

2 Related Work

In *'Straight thinking straight from the net – On the web- based intelligent talking toy development'* by Rzepka et al. explored early stages of smart toy development, and limitation on functionalities; and how to integrate the use of Internet searches to improve language processing functionalities of smart toys. The theme is design three toy engines modules capable of: unlimited talking, emotional recognizing, and moral behavior analyzer. Their goal is to design an inexpensive humanoid which could talk with children in a more mature manner than current talking toys at that time. The author's main work focuses developing an algorithm capable of finding satisfactory semantic online for a conversational agent which has no limitations of topic. The authors work is essential and contributed through building a toy which can talk to children about anything but knowing good from bad or wrong; conversation and affect recognition module which future works can build on. The authors work lacked the ability to provide smart toy engine which provide security or privacy, and does not include adequate sources on in-depth research on current work (Rzepka and Higuchi 2008).

In understanding concept of privacy within Canadian context, the paper *"Two concepts of privacy"* by Hughes researched and discussed current Canadian regulatory statues, the current Canadian court interpretation of privacy infringement and how they impact advancement in ubiquitous collection of data. The author argues that the Canadian legal system interpretation privacy is based either on a civil proceedings or criminal proceedings. The author highlights the steep advancement of technological innovation which has normalized and led to surveillance of everyone, by everyone. The author uncovers struggle by Canadian legislatures, and academics to provide a single definition for the term privacy, address why privacy matters, and when it is violated. These struggles lead to two distinct privacy concepts: dignitary privacy, which is based on the fact the privacy is intrinsic valuable; and resource privacy, which infer privacy as a tool with instrumental value. The theme of the author work is to show inconsistency in how privacy claims are addressed in Canadian court, and provide a coherent explanation of the right of privacy and how it should be applied. The author's work is essential to current research in privacy of smart devices as its highlight for Computer Scientist the challenging information privacy issues facing the judiciary because of advancement in technology. The author provided good sample of real Computer privacy cases, with excellent reliable sources on and how the court adjudicated recent cases on privacy and highlights the inconsistent decision on privacy (Hughes 2015).

Referring to the paper "Privacy protection in pervasive systems: State of the art and technical challenges," Bettini and Riboni argued that there is a challenge pose to data protection and privacy as a result persistent techno- logical innovation allowing collection of huge volumes of data to determine personal behavior pattern, and ascertain location information. The main theme is to address this rising privacy issues and propose innovative technological solution for minimizing privacy infringement, and it negative impact citizenry. The authors reviewed and discussed current privacy protection frameworks across the globe; mainly focusing on European Union approach to privacy as a human right issue, and US approach to privacy as a constitution rights. The authors proposed technological solution including self-selected routing protocols, privacy enhanced search engines, online deletion tools, and privacy enhancing technologies; which includes the use of encryption tools, policy tools, filtering tools and anonymity tools to improve privacy by removing commonly identifiable personal information. This research is an essential resource on privacy on smart devices as it's contribute a global view of privacy, and highlight technological innovation across the globe and current challenges. Although authors relied on good sources; they were unable demonstrate how new privacy framework can address privacy issues raised in various jurisdictions across the globe (Riboni 2015).

Referring to the paper "Privacy leakages in Smart Home wireless technologies" by Sanchez et al. the authors argued that the defacto standard WIFI communication technology used in Smart home appliances, sensors, actuators by it basic nature and design is vulnerable, up to certain limit, to privacy leakages through traffic analysis attacks. Concerns of this technological evolution in relation to the privacy and security of the citizenry appears to be at an embryonic stage. To sustain this claim, the authors explore information leakage vulnerabilities inherent to communication technologies used in Smart Homes and their potential impacts through analyzing the ways in which private information might leak from the wireless protocols. This research is useful to the field of privacy and security of IoT as it demonstrates appliance involve in IoT such as smart toy can be easily be vulnerable as it joins home connectivity. Although the authors used reliable sources; such as previous work in the field, they were unable to provide substantial evidence on how to intercept WIFI communication when adversary machine is not authenticated to the WIFI network. In this case, they fail to demonstrate how they will be practically be able identify various devices connected to the WIFI. They could have easily provided evidence of such attack by using simple WIFI cracking software to demonstrate how adversary can join the WIFI network and start sniffing communication (Sanchez and Satta 2014). This is also important in two facts. For example, if they could identify various devices connected to the WIFI; then in a case of smart toy, and adversary can easily identify a device such as smart toy connected to a Wi-Fi.

Referring to "the digital future a challenge for privacy" by Weber, based on the concern of pervasive big data collection by service providers, the author conducted a survey to consider representative classes of pervasive applications, and identify the requirements they impose in terms of privacy, and trade-off with service quality. The authors review current applications which enable location based services, and conducted privacy threats on geo-social network and sensing applications, and requirement with emphasis on identifying privacy threats and the violation. The theme of work is to discuss technical challenges including, but not limited to, augmenting the awareness of individuals, privacy preferences, and associated economic cost to privacy infringement. Author proposes privacy preservation approaches necessary to be incorporated into new technology. Since smart toys are still an emerging research topic in the market, there are not much research works done in privacy (Weber 2015).

Referring to the paper "There is more to context than location" by Schmidt et al. (1999), the authors discussed the significance of context data in ultra-mobile computing, and provided key context data that are gathered during the use of ultra-mobile device. The authors discuss the primary concern of context-awareness in mobile computing is the awareness of the physical environment surrounding a user and their ultra-mobile device. This concern applies to smart connected toys such a way that similar context data is collected. In recent work, this concern has been addressed by implementation of location-awareness, for instance based on global positioning, or the use of beacons. The authors proposed a working model. Their model, a hierarchically organized feature space for context can be developed. At the top level, authors proposed distinguishing context related to human factors, and context related to the physical environment. The authors proposed further classification into three categories: information on the user (knowledge of habits, emotional state, bio physiological conditions), the user's social environment (co-location of others, social interaction, group dynamics), and the user's tasks (spontaneous activity, engaged tasks, general goals). Authors argued that context related to physical environment is structured into three categories: location (absolute position, relative position, co-location), infrastructure (surrounding resources for computation, communication, task performance, etc.), and physical conditions (noise, light, pressure). According to their model, context can originate from human factors or physical environment, human factors can be categorized into three as user (his knowledge, characteristics, habits, etc.), social environment (social interaction, etc.) and tasks (engaged tasks, general goals, etc.). Physical environment can be also categorized into three as conditions (light, audio, temperature, etc.), infrastructure (surroundings for computation and communication) and location (absolute location, relative location, etc.). The focus of this data model is the context resources. Although this a great work and contributing significant to understanding of context in ubiquitous connected devices, the authors failed to consider context privacy and context interactions and did not raised any concern of context relating to technology to integrate privacy preservation of security of context data gathered.

Referring to the context data model for privacy (Tatli 2006), Tatli argued that context aware application introduces more privacy issues more that location context data. The author expanded on the context data work done by Schmidt et al. (1999), and argued that the more context data available the more increase in the degree of privacy concerns users of context aware application are exposed to. This is significant when the people consider the amount of data smart toy can collect. The author proposed a privacy-aware context data model based on the context data model of Schmidt et al. (1999). This model focuses on context privacy and privacy dependence of context-to-context relations and discusses two main state of context data: (1) protected context; (2) elevated context. The author argues that protected context data focus on information about user and location, and elevated context data focus on user's beliefs, infrastructure, social activity and status. When dealing with smart toy both type of context data applies. The author proposed that there should be a context Interaction in privacy aware model that integrated depicts users protected context data as part of privacy protection which can be blurred when needed based on condition specified by users. The authors failed and classify user specific information such as name, age, address as context data rather that Personal information all which are essential information which are collected by most smart toys.

Referring to the paper "Petimo: Enhanced tangible social networking companion for children" by Cheok et al. (2009), the authors reviewed "Petimo" an interactive robotic toy designed to protect children from potential risks in social networks and the virtual world which helps them to make a safely connected social networking environment. It adds a new form of security to social computing through parental authentication, providing extra safety in making friends by physically touching each other's robot which is a much-preferred form especially by children and natural means of making friends. The authors argue that the concept of Petimo could be extended to any social network thus making it child-safe. As a proof-of-concept a 3D virtual world called "Petimo-World" is developed which includes all the realizable basic features of traditional online social networks. With the system, children experience enhanced relationships with their friends through interactions in the real and virtual worlds by sending personal thoughts and feelings mediated by their robots with haptic, and visual. This is a significant contribution in designing safe smart connected toys. Unfortunately, it works great in cultures or controlled spaces such as schools where there is a great degree of physical face to face interaction amongst children. Mostly in North America, smart toys are not allowed on schools and the culture of significant face to face interaction has diminish significantly. Such culture and the inability to create such control environment for can be problematic for this solution. Secondly there are other aspect of safety and privacy including and not limited to context data and how it is stored which the authors did not discussed.

To continue with exploration of solution to privacy and safety concerns of smart connected toys (Child 2006), the paper "Rule value reinforcement learning for cognitive agents" by Child and Stathis discussed RVRL (Rule Value Reinforcement Learning) is a new algorithm, which extends an existing learning framework that models the environment of a situated agent using a probabilistic rule representation. The algorithm attaches values to learned rules by adapting reinforcement learning. Structure captured by the rules is used to form a policy. The resulting rule values represent the utility of taking an action if the rule's conditions are present in the agent's current percept. Advantages of the new framework are demonstrated, through examples in a predator-prey environment conditions. This rule value approach can be embedded into the design of smart connected toys to help with embedding privacy policy within smart connected toys.

Referring to the paper "Smart toys: brave new world?" by D'Hooge et al. (2000), authors argue that technology is changing the way children play. It raises the spectra if we should be excited or worried about the introduction of technology into children's toys. The authors sample a panel of smart toy experts examined the advantages and disadvantages of technologically-enhanced play and will discuss potential psychological and developmental consequences of electronic play things.

Furthermore, the authors explore how to evaluate smart toys and how to create usability guidelines for high-tech toys. The authors did not discuss detail privacy and security implication of integration of high tech toys into children life. In looking at smart toys, privacy and safety consideration should be incorporated into any evaluation of selecting smart toys for school.

Referring to the paper "Steps Toward Child-Designed Interactive Stuffed Toys" by Huang et al. (2011), the authors made the case that within the past decade, computationally-enhanced toys have become a staple of children's environments in large part due to the small size, robust operation, and low cost of embedded computing that enables computers (and associated electronic devices) to be included within toys of all descriptions. The authors argue that more recently, a variety of powerful technologies have emerged so that children can design their own computational artifacts: that is, small (and inexpensive) processors, sensors, and actuators have been developed that are well-suited to combination with "soft" materials such as textiles. This paper describes Plushbot, a system-in-development that allows children to create their own plush toys and stuffed animals, and to include computational enhancements within the toys that they create. Thus, Plushbot represents a step toward expanding children's creative design of their own interactive, computationally-enhanced characters. The paper describes the current state of the Plushbot software, shows a sample project created with the system, and describes plans for upcoming pilot tests with the system. This paper contributes significant to important element of smart toys "DIY" which can be far dangerous as no consideration are giving to potential easy data breach as no consideration of security is giving during the designing and building of these toys. The authors failed to discuss any mechanism of preserving children data.

Referring to the paper "Can (and should) Hello Barbie Keep a Secret" by Jones (2016), the author argues that the growing proliferation of connected devices in various environments offers an increasing number of opportunities for minors to create and share personal data. The author's analysis looks specifically at the privacy of children interacting with Hello Barbie, a new smart toy from Mattel. This is important and controversial because Hello Barbie can collect, store, and process the information from children. The author assesses Hello Barbie across three fronts. First, the author de-blacks box the technology by testing its interactive capabilities – can Hello Barbie keep a secret? Will she respect privacy when asked or suggest otherwise? How is the information presented in the online dashboard for adult oversight? To situate Hello Barbie in the larger and ongoing conversation surrounding child privacy, the author next discusses Hello Barbie in relation to three other toys designed for children's interaction: Teddy Ruxpin, Elf on the Shelf, and Furby. Finally, the author argues that smart connected toys such as hello Barbie should be able to keep secret and should be built to do so; and as a product specifically geared toward children, higher or different standards should be established for the collection, safeguard, and use of data. This paper provides tangible contribution to the research area into smart toys safe guarding data. It analyzes the toy itself and provides concrete evidence on the current capabilities.

Unfortunately, It lacks proposing a design and methodologies on how a real world propose solution of keeping data secrete can be deployed into the toys.

Referring to the paper "Feature" by Jiang and Wang (2016), the authors research surround computer vision research aims to enable computer to recognize images as easily as human. Author argues that human can segregate target from its surrounding environment, which is associated with human memory mechanism. However, it is not quite clear about how the visual images are stored and retrieved in the human brain. The author introduces the REM (Retrieving Effective from Memory) model into image learning and recognition and study how a computer can learn and recognize visual images as human do. First, the feature vector of the visual image is extracted by the local binary pattern (LBP) method. Then the probe image is matched in parallel to the studied images. Finally, the author uses Bayesian decision is used to calculate the likelihood ratio between the probe image feature vector and that of each studied image. If this ratio is greater than value 1, the probe image is thought to have been studied and match with the studied image with the maximal likelihood. Experimental results show that the REM model can gain good recognition performance not only in the classification of the same object with small. This can be significant contribution in image identification for smart toys processing image.

Referring to the paper "Integration of speech recognition and machine translation in computer-assisted translation" by Khadivi and Ney (2008), the authors argues that parallel integration of automatic speech recognition (ASR) models and statistical machine translation (MT) models is an unexplored research area in comparison to the large amount of works done on integrating them in series. Parallel integration of these models is possible when we have access to the speech of a target language text and to its corresponding source language text, like a computer-assisted translation system. The authors' observation is that only a few methods for integrating ASR models with MT models in parallel have been studied. The authors systematically studied several different translation models in the context of the best list rescoring. The authors carried out on experiment on two tasks conducting ASR vocabulary between languages: English-to-German with an ASR vocabulary size of 17K words, and Spanish-to-English with an ASR vocabulary of 58Kwords. For the best method, the MT models reduce the ASR word error rate by a relative of 18% and 29% on the 17K and the 58K tasks, respectively. Index tasks: English-to-German with an ASR vocabulary size of 17K words, and Spanish-to-English with an ASR vocabulary of 58Kwords. For the best method, the MT models reduce the ASR word error rate by a relative of 18% and 29% on the 17K and the 58K tasks, respective. This research contributes significantly in developing solution for parental management of discussion of the child and the Barbie. Does Barbie speak other languages and who will language processing impact any solution proposed to identify phrases which out of scope for children in their interaction with the smart toys.

In a recent research "Toys that Listen: A Study of Parents, Children, and Internet-Connected Toys" (Mcreynolds and Hubbard 2017), the authors conducted interviews with parent-child pairs in which the participants interacted with Internet connected toys (Hello Barbie and CogniToys Dino), shedding light on children's expectations of the toys' "intelligence" and parents' privacy concerns and expectations for parental controls. The author's goal use empirical investigation of parents' and children's interactions with these toys, and their attitudes about privacy of connected toys. Authors were able to deduce from their experiment that children were often unaware that others might be able to hear what was said to the toy, and that some parents draw connections between the toys and similar tools not intended as toys (e.g., Siri, Alexa) with which their children already interact in order help inform the future designers of interactive connected toys and gadget and advise policy makers on risk and privacy implication (Mcreynolds and Hubbard 2017) These researches provided a base understanding of certain assumption of privacy regarding smart connected toys. This works fell short on discussing further significant privacy breaches and other serious privacy and safety issues within the public discourse. Also, although the authors recognize implicit gap in children own expectation of privacy from their parent, authors did not analyze this problem deeply and proposed any common way of provision children their individual privacy with the SCT children get older.

3   Proposed Conceptual Model

In all the discussion above, several avenues can be explored to address the privacy and safety concern regarding SCT. The goal here is to build a privacy preservation framework (Fig. 3) which will address these issues of privacy and safety without impeding on advances in the functionalities of the SCTs, or its capacity as a conversational agent to establish trust with a child or even his/her parent. The privacy preservation framework includes a *context data model* and a *privacy preserving engine*. In this case *data context model* is an abstract model that organizes elements of data and standardizes how they relate to one another and to properties of the related entities in SCTs based on eXtensible Markup Language (XML). Further the privacy preserving engine is based on the Internet Engineering Task Force (IETF)'s Policy Framework Architecture (PFA) (Fig. 4) for managing toy computing services and extending the traditional services modelling techniques with safety guarantees by means of a privacy policy specification language to support context-dependent policies in XML. The privacy preservation framework is depicted by Pedri-Nets to automatically identify offensive content intended for storage or transmission, tag, classify, alerts, and secure delete content.

In constructing the privacy engine, the sole goal is to provide an integrated framework which encompass all aspect of security including confidentiality, integrity of data, and access to data to ascertain that none of these requirements can be compromise leading to privacy breach of SCT user's data (either context data or directly created data). Figure 3, the privacy preservation framework; include standard real life situational environment and neighboring devices zone. This is the physical and social environment of the SCT and includes similar SCT devices, and online connectable device such as WiFi. Within this zone, context data such as

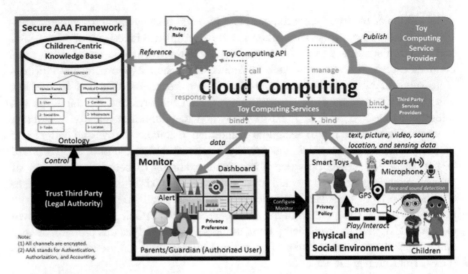

Fig. 3 Privacy preservation framework

The Internet Engineering Task Force (IETF)'s Policy Framework Architecture (PFA)

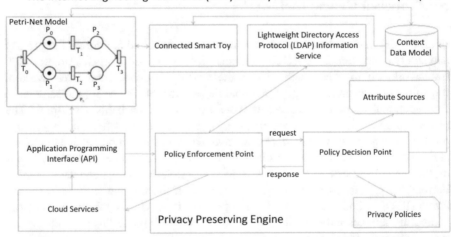

Fig. 4 IETF policy framework architecture

geo-location, original demographic registration information (name, age, gender, and address), directly created interaction data, and activity data is available. Expected types of data, but not limited, interaction, captured data by the SCT through microphone, camera, etc. The SCT will be generally equipped with camera, microphone, GPS, and sensors for face and sound detection which allows the device to create and collect such data. Generally, the SCT manufacturer provides external services through cloud services outside the immediate environment of the SCT. This allows data to be exchanges or sent across from the SCT to the cloud. Information SCT my exchange includes but not limited to text, picture, video, sound (voice), and location and sensing data to the SCT manufactured services provider. Generally, they may be other information which can gathered and inferred from SCT involved prior activity including historical data on the child such as SCT moves around. Within this zone tremendous amount of information are gathered, exchanged and easily shared with other SCT or designated SCT manufactured connected cloud services. Within this zone, we will implement privacy policy framework which is autonomously enforced, and ensures that data all data exchanges between the SCT and cloud services are encrypted. Such policy enforcement will put into place security control best practice including and not limited to Access Control, Integrity enforcement, no repudiation, and encryption which prevent data breach. The privacy policy enforcement ensures that there is a secure channel to allow the SCT communicate with SCT manufacture cloud infrastructure setup. The reason why such is needed is data autonomous policy enforcement with security control enables that collected data, both directly and from within other applications (e.g. sensitive data can be collected such as a user's registration information, contact list, calendar, and another list) is secure.

The SCT usually will communicate with other network entities to carry services to SCT manufacture cloud solution as describe above. The idea here is prior to any communication to the cloud service provider, a parent/guardian will have configured a privacy preference file which then in incorporated into the privacy policy as discussed above. This attest that the guardian will be in charge to monitor child activities and be alerted in case any of the rules in the privacy policy is breached. Generally, a child (data subject) is associated with an identity, but the parent is the data owner and control access (read, write, modify) and use of the data other than privilege granted to the child. It is because context data including location data, it can lead to identification of the child and his or her location. It is incumbent on the system to provide a level of initial preference which is on default lockdown. This means that the SCT cannot be used, until the preference file is configured for access by the parent.

The last two component Secure AAA framework, and Services Rules for Cloud Computing makes sure the privacy breach does not occur when data moves into the cloud services providers' infrastructure. The cloud services provider has an applied privacy rules which works like the description of the privacy policy. The cloud service provider applies a secure Authentication, Authorization and Accounting framework to ascertain that privacy is maintain. This means for Authentication implementation we adopt current Information Security Industry best practices for user authentication. For example, a good combination of current password policy coupled of multifactor authentication. The password policy can take into consideration, complex password, password expiry, etc. The Authorization and Accounting deal with addressing the need to make sure the right person can access user data. The goal of the set of protection to prevent security violations leading to privacy breach based on good security design principle such as: Economy of mechanism (Keep the design as simple and small as possible); Fail-safe defaults (default situation is lack of access); Complete mediation (access to every object must be checked for authority); Separation of privilege (Where feasible, a protection mechanism that requires two keys); Compromise recording (reliably record that a compromise of information); and Least privilege (operate using the least rights required to accomplish task) (Saltzer 2017).

The Internet Engineering Task Force (IETF)'s Policy framework architecture implementation Fig. 4, will allow modeling of different privacy state using Petri-Net, during SCT various interaction. The modeling of the privacy states will take into consideration context data gathers from the SCT environment. Within this design, the privacy engine will provide policy enforcement point on cloud services and Lightweight Directory Access Protocol information service based on request and response approved privacy policy within the engine. The sole goal is to minimize any potential privacy breaches of the SCT both within SCT connected network or data request from the cloud services.

4   Conclusion

The child protection is not just the "protection of children from violence, exploitation, abuse, and neglect." It should also include protection children data or any related information that can compromise a child safety. Protecting the childs' data should be considered by the SCT manufacture through design process, and must be demanded by parents. Privacy by Design (PbD) is an approach to systems engineering which takes privacy into account throughout the whole engineering process (Cavoukian 2016). The PbD approach is characterized by proactive rather than reactive measures. It anticipates and prevents privacy invasive events before they happen. The PbD does not wait for privacy risks to materialize, nor does it offer remedies for resolving privacy infractions once they have occurred, which aims to prevent them from occurring. In short, PbD comes before-the-fact, not after (Cavoukian 2016). Another approach is Banning subject to permission. According to this principle, companies may not collect, use or save personal data in principle unless the legislator has permitted this as an exception situations or the minor himself permits it by giving consent. Further the implementation will be consideration of data economy. Data economy specifies that companies may only ever collect just as much data as is required to fulfil a purpose. For example, completing a participation form for a competition does not mean minors should also have to provide information on hobbies, preferences and similar personal circumstances. Finally, consent purpose must be fulfilled. Even if the company may legally collect and use certain data for a purpose, they cannot use the same data for other purpose. Lastly in cases where affected data is shared, there should be a degree of transparency which allows user to trace which data a company is using for and which purpose to whom the company is passing on this data.

References

Anikweze GU (2014) The relevance of fabric toys in childhood. Am Int J Res Humant Art Soc Sci 2014:55–62

Cavoukian A (2016) Privacy by design: the 7 foundational principles. IAB, Toronto. Retrieve from https://www.ipc.on.ca/wp-content/uploads/Resources/7foundationalprinciples.pdf

Cheok AD (2009) Petimo: enhanced tangible social networking companion for children. In: Proceedings of the international conference on advances in computer entertainment technology – ACE, pp 411–412

Child C (2006) Rule value reinforcement learning for cognitive agents. In: Proceedings of the fifth international joint conference on autonomous agents and multiagent systems, p 792

D'Hooge HD (2000) Smart toys: brave new world? . CHI '00 Extended abstracts on human factors in computing systems, 247–248

HealthCanada (2017) www.hc-sc.gc.ca. Retrieved from www.hc-sc.gc.ca: http://www.hc-sc.gc.ca/cps-spc/pubs/indust/toys-jouets/index-eng.php

Huang Y (2011) Steps toward child-designed interactive stuffed toys. In: Proceedings of the 10th international conference on interaction design and children – IDC, pp 165–168

Hughes RL (2015) Two concepts of privacy. Comput Law Secur Rev, ScienceDirect 31(4):5

Hung PC (2015) Mobile services for toy computing, the Springer International Series on Applications and Trends in Computer Science. Springer International Publishing, Cham

Jiang Y (2016) Feature. In: 2016 12th World Congress on Intelligent Control and Automation (WCICA), Guilin, China, pp 3167–3171

Jones ML (2016) Can (and should) Hello Barbie keep a secret? IEEE

Kara NC (2013) Investigating the activities of children toward a smart storytelling toy. J Educ Technol Soc 16(1):28–43

Khadivi S (2008) Integration of speech recognition and machine translation in computer-assisted translation. In: IEEE transactions on audio, speech and language processing, 1551–1564

LaMonica M (2015) Mobile apps reshape toys and learning. 18 April 2012. [Online]. Available: CNET – http://www.cnet.com/news/mobile-apps-reshape-toys-and-learning/

Mcreynolds E, Hubbard S (2017) Toys that listen : a study of parents, children , and internet-connected toys. CHI

Rafferty L (2015) Location privacy framework for mobile toy computing. Master Dissertation. University of Ontario Institute of Technology, Oshawa

Rafferty LB (2015) Toy computing background: mobile services for toy computing. Master Dissertation. University of Ontario Institute of Technology. Springer International Publishing, Oshawa

Riboni CB (2015) Privacy protection in pervasive systems: state of the art and technical challenges. Pervasive Mob Comput 17:159–174

Rzepka R, Higuchi S (2008) Straight thinking straight from the net – on the web-based intelligent talking toy development. In: Proceedings of the IEEE International Conference on Systems, Man, and Cybernetics, pp 2172–2176

Saltzer (2017) mit.edu. Retrieved from web.mit.edu: http://web.mit.edu/Saltzer/www/publications/protection/Basic.html

Sanchez I, Satta R (2014) Privacy leakages in Smart Home wireless technologies. In: International Carnahan Conference on Security Technology, 1–6

Schmidt AB (1999) There is more to context than location. Computers and Graphics (Pergamon) 23(6):893–901. doi:https://doi.org/10.1016/S0097-8493(99)00120-X

Shop FT (2016) Forgotten toy shop – history of toys & games. Retrieved from Forgotten Toy Shop – History of Toys & Games: https://www.theforgottentoyshop.co.uk/pages/history-of-toys-games

Smith R (2016) Family Online Safety Institute -connected toys and privacy. What good digital parents should know. Retrieved from Family Online Safety Institute: https://www.fosi.org/good-digital-parenting/connected-toys-and-privacy-what-parents-should-kno/

Tatli EI (2006) Context data model for privacy. PRIME Project Standardization Workshop, 1–6
Weber RH (2015) The digital future – a challenge for privacy. Comput Law Secur, ScienceDirect 31(2):Z234–Z242
WeLiveSecurity (2016) 5 of the most devastating data breaches of 2015. WeLiveSecurity

Printed in the United States
By Bookmasters